CONNECT

CONNECT

THE PATIENT'S VOICE:

LISTENING, LEADING, AND TRANSFORMING CARE

MICHAEL WINKLEMAN

patientX®

patientX

Published by PatientX PO Box 1655, Sioux Falls, South Dakota, 57101 www.patientxagency.com

The patient and family member quotes in this book are drawn from real interviews, reviews, and surveys conducted over more than a decade. Names and identifying details have been changed to protect privacy. Ages are approximate and are used for attribution purposes only.
This book is intended for educational and informational purposes and does not constitute medical advice.

Paperback ISBN: 979-8-9954434-0-7 eBook ISBN: 979-8-9954434-1-4 Audiobook ISBN: 979-8-9954434-2-1
Library of Congress Control Number: 2026910550

Book design: Valeria Muñoz , Cover design: Valeria Muñoz, Editor: Kimberly Winkleman, Associate Editor: Mariana Martinez, Editorial Coordinator: Brittany Jones, Digital Promoter: Alejandra Rodas.

First Edition
Printed in the United States of America.

DEDICATION

To the provider who finally listened when I was twenty-one — you planted the seed for everything that followed.

To my mom, whose courage taught me that patients don't stop fighting just because the system stops paying attention.

To my dad, whose misdiagnosis taught our family what's at stake when connection breaks down — and what's possible when someone looks closer.

To my wife and kids, who gave me the space and the reason to keep doing this work.

To God, for every exam room door that opened.

And to every patient who trusted me with their story — this book is yours.

"LISTENING IS LEADERSHIP. WHEN PROVIDERS AND TEAMS HONOR THE PATIENT'S VOICE, THEY IGNITE HEALING NOT ONLY FOR PATIENTS BUT FOR THEMSELVES."

- MICHAEL WINKLEMAN

"WHEN WE TRULY LISTEN TO PATIENTS, WE DON'T JUST HEAL THEIR BODIES, WE RESTORE THEIR DIGNITY, TRUST, AND HOPE. THAT'S WHERE THE FUTURE OF HEALTHCARE BEGINS."

- MICHAEL WINKLEMAN

TABLE OF CONTENTS

FOREWORD

In my life, I have witnessed both despair and miracles at the hands of those who chose this calling. I have seen families shattered by a rushed word, and I have seen hope restored by a single act of presence and compassion. That tension — between despair and miracles — often comes down to one thing: connection.

My own family's journey taught me this lesson again and again. When I was twenty-one, I struggled with constant dizziness and nausea. I saw provider after provider, each giving a different diagnosis: possible brain cancer, possible heart disease, and other possibilities. Nothing fit. I worked, I endured, and I waited. Then someone truly listened, looked deeper, and recognized the symptoms of Meniere's disease. The difference wasn't more tests. It was listening.

I saw it again with my mom, who was vibrant and tireless until her health began to decline. She was dismissed as a hypochondriac, her concerns brushed aside. Later, we discovered the truth: a hole in her aortic valve, a genetic condition that should have been caught. What she needed wasn't just medical knowledge — it was someone willing to slow down and hear her story.

And again, with my dad. He was told in an ER that he had pancreatic cancer and likely only months to live. My mom was handed a brochure on death and dying.

Our family lived under the shadow of despair until a second opinion revealed it wasn't cancer at all, but a cyst. What changed our lives wasn't technology. It was the courage of a team that looked closer and connected with him as a person, not a prognosis.

These aren't isolated examples. This was years of oversight, across multiple experiences, just within one family. Multiply that across thousands of families, and you begin to see the true weight of disconnection in healthcare. This isn't about blame. It's about opportunity.

For more than a decade, I've had the privilege of interviewing hundreds of patients and healthcare providers. I've listened in waiting rooms. I've sat in consultation rooms. I've stood inside surgery suites, photographing live procedures while hearing the conversations that unfold there. I've watched a surgeon pause mid-procedure to explain what was happening to a nervous family member over the phone. I've watched a receptionist completely change a patient's day with nothing more than eye contact and a warm voice. And I've watched patients sit alone in hallways, invisible, while the system moved around them. Every encounter, every story, has shaped this book.

Healthcare providers are my heroes. My family and friends are my heart. That's why this work has become my mission and my passion.

One thing I want to be clear about before we go further: this book is for everyone who touches a patient's experience. Not just the physician in the exam room. Not just the nurse at the bedside. This is for the person who answers the phone on a Monday morning when a scared patient calls for the first time. It's for the medical assistant who rooms the patient and sets the emotional tone before the doctor ever walks in. It's for the transporter who wheels someone down a hallway in silence and chooses whether to fill that silence with warmth or let it echo. It's for the housekeeper who enters a room during the hardest moment of someone's day.

It's for the billing specialist who becomes the last voice a patient hears from your organization — the person who determines whether the final impression is care or confusion. It's for the scheduler, the lab tech, the receptionist, the IT team that designs the portal, and the leader whose decisions shape whether any of this is even possible.

Every person in a healthcare organization is either building trust or eroding it. There is no neutral role. You all shape whether someone feels cared for — or processed. And this book is for every one of you.

I know these stories will infuriate many of you — and they should. Ask yourself: did these moments guide us to connect with patients and truly listen, or were they brushed off as brief discussions? How can we change this? How can we create a culture where listening is as natural as breathing? Some of you already do this instinctively, but even the best of us need reminders.

We are all human, and so are our patients. And we must never forget: we are all patients ourselves. I've even heard doctors admit they dislike going to their own yearly health checks. Why is that? What does it say about the way we deliver and experience care?

The truth is, connection isn't a luxury. It's the foundation. Patients want to feel seen, heard, and remembered. Providers want to make a difference that goes beyond charts and checklists.

When those voices meet — when connection bridges the gap — extraordinary things happen.

This book is both a guide and a reminder. A guide for how to weave connection into the everyday realities of care, and a reminder of why you chose this work in the first place.

Connection doesn't cost more time. It doesn't require more staff. It doesn't demand another piece of technology. It just asks that we show up — with presence, with humanity, and a willingness to listen.

Healthcare is filled with pressures: productivity, compliance, metrics, and finances. But at its heart, it's filled with something more powerful: you. The hands that steady a child, the eyes that meet a patient in fear, the words that deliver not just information but dignity.

My hope is that this book uplifts you. That it reminds you of the miracles you've already created and the ones still waiting to be born through your work. That it encourages you to keep listening, keep connecting, and keep leading with heart.

Because the greatest medicine patients will ever receive isn't just what you prescribe. It's the connection you create.

And here's what I've learned after a decade of watching, listening, and standing in those rooms: Listening is the intervention. Everything else follows from there.

PART I – THE PSYCHOLOGY OF PATIENTS & BUILDING THE BEST EXPERIENCE

Before we hear from patients in their own words, we need to understand what's happening beneath the surface — why these moments matter so much, and what's at stake when we get them right or wrong. This section is the *"why."* Part II is the *"what."* And waiting at the end of this book is a 30-day challenge that will change how you show up in every room you enter.

"Listening first isn't about standing back. It's about choosing to see the person in front of you before you ever open the chart."

#1
INTRODUCTION: LISTENING FIRST

When patients walk into a clinic or hospital, they don't just bring their symptoms. They carry their entire story — their fears, their hopes, the argument they had with their spouse that morning, the worry about whether the bill will be affordable, the memory of how their father was treated in a hospital twenty years ago. They bring their whole lives, condensed into the fragile moment of sitting in a waiting room or lying on an exam table.

Providers carry stories too. They walk into a room with the residue of the last patient's tears still on their mind, the endless alerts from the electronic health record, the worry about being behind schedule, or the fatigue of an on-call night that stretched too long. Between these two worlds — the patient's and the provider's — there's a meeting point. A moment. A chance.

I've spent years asking patients one question:

"What does it feel like when a provider truly connects with you?"

The answers were striking in their simplicity. They didn't ask for miracles. They didn't ask for flawless care or cutting-edge technology.

They asked to be seen. They asked to be heard. They asked for honesty, kindness, and hope.

Those requests aren't *"soft"* skills. They're deeply rooted in human psychology. They're the things that determine whether a patient feels safe enough to tell the whole story, to ask the embarrassing question, or to follow through on the treatment plan. They're also the things that determine whether a provider rediscovers the joy of medicine or sinks deeper into burnout.

I remember standing in an exam room, as a physician sat down, leaned forward, and simply said,

"Tell me everything."

The patient — a man in his sixties who had been stoic and guarded with the nurse — exhaled visibly and began talking. Really talking. That physician didn't do anything complicated. He just chose to listen before he diagnosed.

Listening first isn't about being passive. It's about choosing to see the person in front of you before you ever open the chart. It's about pausing, just for a moment, to let connection become the first step in care.

"Patients show up already carrying so much. They walk in hoping someone will notice what they can't put into words."

#2 THE HUMAN SIDE OF VULNERABILITY

A nurse once told me, *"The hardest part of my job isn't the medicine. It's knowing that every person who walks into my room is scared, even when they don't show it."* Anyone who works in healthcare understands this truth. Patients rarely arrive as their strongest selves. They come exhausted, anxious, confused, hopeful, hurting, or trying their best to hold it all together.

And yet, when patients recall their healthcare experiences, their stories almost always return to one theme: vulnerability.

"I felt exposed in that gown."
"I didn't want to say I was scared."
"I hoped they could see how much I needed reassurance."
"I don't want to be judged."
"How will I afford this?"

Vulnerability isn't loud. It doesn't always show up in tears or shaking hands. Often, it hides behind polite smiles, quiet nods, or the phrase every provider hears: *"I'm fine."* But beneath those words is a person handing over control of their body, future, and safety. Trusting a stranger to help them make sense of it all.

Most providers never see the full weight their patients carry. The years of symptoms brushed off. The worry whispered in the car. The long nights of online searching and now AI searches. The fear of a diagnosis that changes everything. Patients show up already carrying so much. They walk in hoping someone will notice what they can't put into words.

Here's the quiet reality: providers carry vulnerability too. You shoulder impossible schedules, heavy emotional loads, heartbreaking conversations, and expectations no human could perfectly meet.

You move from room to room balancing compassion with pace, expertise with uncertainty, empathy with efficiency. It's not that you don't care. It's that the system rarely gives you space to show it.

I've seen this firsthand. I once watched a physician walk out of a room where she'd just delivered a terminal diagnosis, lean against the hallway wall for three seconds with her eyes closed, take a breath, and walk into the next room with a smile. No one checked on her. No one asked how she was holding up. Providers are human too — and that humanity is an asset, not a weakness.

This is where connection becomes powerful. Vulnerability isn't something to fix. It's something to honor. When providers acknowledge the human side of a patient's fear — even with a simple phrase like

"I know this is overwhelming" —

it changes the room. Patients exhale. They soften. They feel safe enough to speak honestly, which in turn helps you treat them more effectively.

And here's the most encouraging part: honoring vulnerability doesn't take more time. It takes intention. A softer tone. A pause before rushing into the next question. A genuine moment of reassurance that says,

"You're not alone in this."

In the end, vulnerability is the meeting place between patient and provider. It's where healing relationships begin. And sometimes, one small acknowledgment of someone's fear becomes the moment they remember long after the appointment is over.

"For just this moment, let the person in front of you be the only story that matters."

#3 WHY PRESENCE IS HARD (BUT WORTH IT)

A physician once confessed:

"I want to give my patients my full attention, but the system pulls me in five directions at once."

Any provider knows the truth of this. There's always a chart to complete, a message to answer, a question waiting in the hallway.

And yet, when patients describe what mattered most to them, their stories return to a single word: presence.

"She made me feel like the only person in the room."
"He looked at me instead of the screen."
"For once, I didn't feel rushed."

The clock doesn't measure presence. Attention does. A provider may spend only three minutes with a patient, but if those three minutes are undivided — eyes up, listening, leaning in — they expand in the patient's memory. Conversely, fifteen distracted minutes feel hollow, even careless.

I learned this lesson watching a pediatrician in a busy clinic. She was running forty-five minutes behind.

When she finally entered the room, she sat down on the floor next to a four-year-old, asked about his dinosaur shirt, and listened to the mom's concerns without once glancing at the clock. The whole encounter lasted maybe six minutes. Afterward, the mom told me,

"That's why we drive forty minutes to see her. She makes us feel like the only family she's seeing today."

Six minutes. That's all it took. Think about the last time someone gave you their full attention. No phone, no glances at the door, no multitasking. It probably felt rare, almost startling. For patients, who often arrive anxious and uncertain, that kind of attention is the medicine they need.

Here's the paradox: presence doesn't require more time. It requires focus. A pause at the doorway before entering. A deep breath to set aside the chaos. Choosing, just for that encounter, to let the person in front of you be the only story that matters.

Providers sometimes worry that presence will slow them down. But more often, the opposite is true. Patients who feel heard speak more openly, ask fewer repetitive questions, and leave more confident in the plan. Presence saves time because it builds trust.

In the end, presence isn't perfection. It's not about never being distracted or never running behind. It's about moments. And sometimes, a single moment of genuine presence is what the patient carries with them long after the visit is over.

"Waiting isn't dead time. It's one of the most important parts of the care experience."

#4 THE WEIGHT OF WAITING

If you want to understand the patient's perspective of waiting, sit in a gown in a silent exam room for twenty minutes. Count the seconds. Listen to the clock. Notice how quickly your thoughts turn dark.

For providers, waiting is often invisible. A patient waits in one room while another requires urgent attention, while a lab result comes back, while the provider documents notes. Ten minutes here, fifteen there — it feels like part of the rhythm of care. But for patients, waiting is never neutral. Time stretches under the weight of anxiety. Silence amplifies fear. What feels like a scheduling hiccup to the provider becomes a story the patient is writing in real time: They've forgotten me. Something must be wrong. I don't matter here.

I remember a patient who put it plainly:

"The longer I waited, the smaller I felt."

That wasn't about actual minutes on a clock — it was about the silence of being left in uncertainty.

I saw the opposite once in a clinic that was running an hour behind. A medical assistant walked into each waiting room, knelt down to eye level, and said,

"I'm sorry for the wait. Dr. [name] is with a patient who needed extra time, and she'll be with you soon. Can I get you some water?"

Every single patient I talked to afterward mentioned that moment. Not the wait. The acknowledgement.

Waiting doesn't just happen in exam rooms. It happens in lobbies, in phone queues, in the days between a scan and its results.

And each kind of waiting carries its own psychological weight. Patients often describe these stretches as the hardest part — not because of the delay itself, but because of the absence of reassurance.

The paradox, again, is that providers can't always eliminate waiting. But they can transform it. A receptionist who greets with warmth, a nurse who offers an update, a provider who apologizes sincerely for the delay — all these turn waiting from abandonment into acknowledgment. Even something as small as a hallway glance that says

"I see you" shifts the experience.

Waiting, then, isn't dead time. It's a critical part of the care experience. If ignored, it erodes trust before the visit even begins. If acknowledged, it becomes a moment of connection that carries forward into the encounter.

"What makes the first minute so powerful isn't anything complicated. It's just a moment of genuine attention."

#5
THE FIRST MINUTE MATTERS

We decide who we trust faster than we realize. Research suggests people form trait impressions from a face in as little as 100 milliseconds, and added time often increases confidence more than it changes the initial judgment. In healthcare, that first minute isn't a courtesy — it's the foundation of the entire encounter.

Patients often describe these opening moments with surprising clarity.

"He didn't look up when I walked in."
"She smiled and said my name. I felt safe right away."

The way a provider enters a room, the first words spoken, the tone of voice, even posture — these details shape whether a patient opens up or shuts down.

Consider two scenarios. In the first, a doctor rushes in, eyes already on the computer, typing while asking,

"What brings you in today?"

The patient hesitates, unsure whether to interrupt the typing with something as vulnerable as fear.

In the second, the doctor sits down, makes eye contact, and says,

"I'm glad you're here. Tell me what's going on."

The same amount of time, but an entirely different foundation.

I've watched hundreds of these moments through the years. The ones that go well almost always have one thing in common: the provider paused. Even for two seconds. They made eye contact before they made a clinical assessment. They acknowledged the human before they addressed the chart.

That first minute communicates three silent questions every patient asks: **Am I safe here? Do I matter? Will you listen?** When the answers feel like yes, the patient relaxes. Honesty comes easier. Compliance improves. When the answers feel like no, the encounter becomes guarded, even adversarial.

What makes the first minute so powerful isn't anything complicated. It's just a moment of genuine attention. A pause to set down the clipboard. A greeting that signals warmth. These small gestures echo throughout the visit.

Providers sometimes underestimate their own influence in this moment. But patients rarely do. They remember. They retell the story. They carry it into how they feel about the entire system. The first minute matters more than most of us realize.

"Healing often starts the moment someone feels seen, comforted, and not alone."

#6 TOUCH BEYOND THE PHYSICAL

Touch is one of the oldest forms of healing. A hand on the shoulder, a gentle reassurance — these acts go back centuries. Yet in modern healthcare, *"touch"* is more than physical contact. It's an emotional presence, the felt sense that someone is with you in your vulnerability.

Not every patient welcomes physical touch, and not every provider is comfortable offering it. But every patient longs for connection. Sometimes touch is literal: the nurse who adjusts a blanket with care, the physician who places a steadying hand during difficult news. Sometimes it's entirely non-physical: a tone of voice that conveys compassion, the words

"That must be so hard,"

or even silence held without rushing to fill it. Patients consistently tell me they remember these small moments of human connection more than the clinical details. One woman described how her doctor simply leaned forward, tilted his head, and said softly,

"I can see how much this weighs on you." Later she told me, *"I left feeling seen and supported — just from the way he listened."*

I saw one of the most powerful examples of this in a pre-op room. A surgical nurse noticed that a patient's wife was gripping his hand so tightly her knuckles were white. The nurse didn't say anything profound. She pulled up a chair next to the wife, put her hand on the woman's arm, and sat there quietly for about thirty seconds. The wife's shoulders dropped. Her grip softened. Later, she told me that moment meant more to her than anything anyone said that day.

"She didn't try to fix my fear. She just sat in it with me."

Science explains why these moments work. Comforting interactions — whether through words, posture, or physical presence — can trigger the release of oxytocin, the hormone that fosters trust and alleviates stress. Touch, in this sense, becomes chemistry. It rewires fear into safety.

Too often, providers think healing lies only in the prescription pad or procedure. But patients know differently. Healing often starts the moment someone feels seen, comforted, and not alone. Touch — physical or emotional — is the bridge.

"Every exam room is full of more than symptoms. It's full of stories."

#7 SEEING THE WHOLE ROOM

A patient walks in carrying the invisible weight of past experiences: a father lost to cancer, a childhood fear of hospitals, an ongoing worry about insurance bills. A provider walks in carrying the stress of missed sleep, the frustration of bureaucracy, or the lingering sadness of delivering bad news an hour earlier.

Both stories enter the room, even if unspoken. And both matter.

Too often, empathy is framed as a one-way street — from provider to patient. But empathy begins with acknowledging that both sides are human. When a provider recognizes their own limits, fatigue, or frustration, they can more consciously set those aside rather than letting them leak into the encounter. And when a provider remembers that a patient brings their own complex story, it prevents reducing them to

"the knee replacement in room three."

One provider described it this way:

"I try to remind myself that I'm stepping into a chapter of their story, not just a case file."

That shift changes everything. It opens the door for compassion instead of judgment, curiosity instead of assumption.

Early in my career of listening to patients, I made the mistake of focusing only on what they said. Over time, I learned to pay attention to what they didn't say — the fidgeting, the downcast eyes, the spouse in the corner who looked like they wanted to speak but didn't.

The exam room is never just about the chief complaint. It's about the marriage that's strained by the illness, the job that might not survive another absence, the child at home who's scared.

Patients can sense when a provider sees only their symptoms. They can also sense when a provider sees them as a whole person. The difference is profound. One makes the patient feel like a chart. The other makes them feel like a human being who matters.

Seeing the whole room isn't about solving everything for everyone in it. It's about recognizing the shared humanity that fills the space. The exam room is never empty of context. The more we acknowledge that, the more real connection becomes.

"Dignity lives in the tone of your voice, your eye contact, and even the pause before you respond."

#8 THE FRAGILITY OF DIGNITY

There are few things in healthcare as fragile as a patient's sense of dignity. It can be preserved or lost in an instant. The simple act of putting on a gown strips away layers of identity. A business leader, a teacher, a mother, a veteran — suddenly they're a patient, exposed and uncertain.

In moments like these, patients read meaning into everything — the tone of your voice, your pacing, your eye contact, even the pause before you respond. A provider who knocks before entering communicates respect. A nurse who carefully adjusts a sheet to preserve modesty conveys care. Conversely, a rushed entrance, a door left ajar, or a conversation spoken over the patient as though they aren't there sends the opposite message: you are an object, not a person.

Patients remember these moments. One man put it bluntly:

"When they talked about me like I wasn't in the room, I felt invisible."

Another described how a nurse who simply called her by her name instead of *"the patient"* restored her sense of self.

I once watched an interaction that stayed with me for years. A surgeon walked into a pre-op area where a patient — a retired Marine — was sitting in a gown, looking smaller than I suspect he'd looked in decades. The surgeon extended his hand and said,

"Thank you for your service, sir. I'm going to take good care of you today."

That man's posture changed in a second. He sat up straighter. He looked the surgeon in the eye. In one sentence, the surgeon had given him back his identity.

Dignity isn't a luxury. It's the foundation that every other act of care rests on.

"You don't have to be an expert in every culture. You just have to be willing to ask."

#9
CULTURE SHAPES CONNECTION

Culture isn't an accessory. It's the lens through which every patient experiences illness, healing, and care. It shapes who gets called first, who makes decisions, how pain is described, what *"good news"* sounds like, and what fear looks like. It shapes whether a patient wants direct answers or gentler pacing, whether they want family present or privacy protected, whether silence means agreement, respect, grief, or discomfort.

That's why culture can't be treated like an afterthought — something reduced to a checkbox, a language preference, or a line in the chart. Patients feel it when their identity is ignored. They feel it when assumptions are made about what they believe, how they live, or what they *"should"* value. And those moments don't just create awkwardness. They create risk. Patients share less. They nod instead of clarifying. They avoid returning.

The good news is that cultural respect doesn't require you to be an expert in every tradition. Most patients aren't asking for perfection. They're asking for curiosity. The simplest question can change the entire encounter. One patient told us,

"She didn't ignore at my beliefs — she asked about them."

That moment didn't just feel polite — it felt protective. Another remembered a doctor who asked how religious fasting might affect treatment timing and dosing.

"He cared about my faith as much as my body,"

the patient said. Those questions signal something deeper than knowledge: I'm not here to judge you. I'm here to understand you.

Culture also extends beyond ethnicity. It includes religion, yes — but also family structure, communication style, military background, rural life, immigration experience, disability, gender roles, trauma history, and the norms people grew up with around authority and medicine. Some patients were raised to never question a clinician. Some were raised to bring the entire family into the decision. Some see illness as private. Others see it as communal. If providers don't make space for these realities, patients are forced to either conform — or conceal.

Respecting culture means asking instead of assuming:

- *"Who do you want involved in decisions?"*
- *"Are there any beliefs or traditions we should consider as we plan care?"*
- *"Are there foods, practices, or routines that matter to you right now?"*
- *"Is there anything about your background that would help me care for you better?"*

These questions don't slow care down. They prevent missteps that cost far more time later — missed understanding, failed plans, unnecessary conflict, avoidable nonadherence.

Respecting culture isn't political correctness. It's safety. It tells patients: you are welcome as you are. And when patients feel welcome, they're more honest, more engaged, and more likely to trust the plan — because the plan finally feels like it was made with their real life in mind.

"Honesty delivered with empathy isn't just the right thing to do. It's part of the healing."

#10
THE POWER OF HONESTY

When patients talk about honesty, their stories are rarely about the facts themselves. They're about how those facts were delivered.

One woman recalled:

"He told me the truth, even though it was hard. But he looked me in the eye and said, 'I'll walk with you through this.' That's what got me through."

Contrast that with the patient who said,

"They avoided telling me until the last second. I felt blindsided. Betrayed."

Honesty isn't about being blunt. It's about being clear, compassionate, and courageous. Patients can endure hard news when they feel supported. What they can't endure is silence, evasion, or false reassurance.

I think about my dad's story often when I write about honesty. He was told in an ER that he had pancreatic cancer. Months to live. My mom was handed a brochure.

The honesty in that room was incomplete — it was a conclusion delivered without the full truth. A second opinion revealed it wasn't cancer at all. What our family needed wasn't softer words. We needed more accurate words, delivered by someone willing to sit with us in the uncertainty instead of rushing to a verdict.

From a human perspective, honesty restores agency. It allows patients to prepare, to plan, to make choices. Even in devastating situations, truth delivered with care creates stability. Without it, patients feel powerless.

Providers sometimes fear that honesty will overwhelm patients. But often, what overwhelms patients is the absence of it. The unknown is heavier than the known. Honesty delivered with empathy isn't just the right thing to do. It's part of the healing.

"Hope does real, measurable things — it lowers stress hormones, strengthens immunity, and builds resilience."

#11
HOW HOPE SHAPES US

Hope isn't fluff. It's medicine. Patients consistently tell us that beyond information, beyond procedures, what they long for is the belief that tomorrow can be better than today.

Hope doesn't mean false promises. It means reframing despair into possibility. It means saying,

"We don't have all the answers yet, but here's what we can do together."

It means pointing to small victories along the way: improved numbers, a step without pain, a night of good sleep.

One patient described how her provider simply said,

"You're stronger than you think."

She carried those words through weeks of treatment. Another recalled being told,

"You're doing better than you realize."

That encouragement became fuel. Science supports what patients know intuitively: hope lowers stress hormones, strengthens immunity, and builds resilience. The body follows where the mind dares to go.

Providers sometimes underestimate how powerful their words are. A casual comment, an encouraging phrase, a vision of life beyond illness — these moments of hope echo long after the visit ends.

Hope isn't sentimental. It's survival.

"Partnership isn't about knowing the same things. It's about valuing each other's voice."

#12 THE PARTNERSHIP PATIENTS CRAVE

For much of history, medicine was characterized by paternalism. Providers prescribed. Patients complied. Questions were limited, and participation was rare. But patients today want something profoundly different: partnership.

Partnership doesn't mean abandoning clinical judgment. It means pairing your knowledge with the patient's lived experience. It means asking,

"What are your goals?" and "How do you feel about this plan?"

It means treating patients as allies in their own healing, not as passive recipients of instructions.

Patients describe partnership as transformative. One man said,

"When they asked me what I thought, I finally felt like a partner, not a project." Another said, "They respected my preferences. That made me trust their expertise even more."

The principle is clear: when patients have a voice, they take more ownership. Compliance turns into commitment. Plans become personal. Healing feels like something shared.

Partnership isn't about knowing the same things. It's about valuing each other's voice. Both voices matter. Both bring something essential to the table.

At its best, partnership communicates the message every patient longs to hear: We are in this together.

"People follow through when the plan feels personal, not transactional."

#13
THE SCIENCE OF REMEMBERING

When patients describe feeling dismissed, the story is often the same:

"I had to tell my story all over again." Or, "They didn't remember me at all."

Those moments sting not because repeating information is inconvenient, but because of what it implies. I'm not memorable here. I don't carry forward. I don't matter enough to be held in mind.

In a system that moves fast, forgetting can feel normal on the inside. But to a patient, forgetting rarely feels neutral. It feels personal. It feels like the relationship resets every time they walk in.

And when a relationship keeps resetting, trust struggles to take root. Patients become guarded. They simplify their story. They stop offering nuance. They stop believing you're tracking the whole picture.

Remembering — even small details — is one of the most powerful ways to dignify a patient. A provider who recalls the name of a spouse, asks about a child's graduation, or remembers what made the patient nervous last time is doing more than demonstrating a good memory.

They're communicating value: You exist here beyond your diagnosis. You were in my thoughts after you left. You're not starting from zero today.

That's why something as small as

"How's your dog doing?"

can land like something enormous. One woman shared how her physician remembered her dog's name from months earlier.

"I felt like a person, not just a file," she said. "I cried in the car after that appointment because I realized how much it meant."

It wasn't the dog. It was the signal: You were paying attention. And you still are.

There's also a practical side. Continuity makes care safer and more effective. When patients don't have to spend their limited emotional energy rebuilding context, they can get to what matters now. The visit becomes less about reconstructing history and more about making progress. Remembering reduces friction. It improves accuracy. It prevents the *"wait, we already did that"* moments that make patients feel like they have to quarterback their own care.

The takeaway is this: memory creates belonging. People follow through when the plan feels personal, not transactional. And they return more confidently because they believe the relationship will still be there when they come back.

Providers don't need perfect recall. Patients aren't grading you on trivia. They're looking for continuity. A quick review of the last plan before you enter. One "life detail" carried forward. One sentence that proves you remember what mattered.

To remember isn't a detail. It's an act of care. It tells a patient: You belong here. And for someone who has felt invisible in healthcare, belonging is healing.

"Underneath everything a patient is thinking, there's one quiet question: Am I safe here?"

#14 SAFETY AS THE FOUNDATION

Underneath everything a patient is thinking, there's one quiet question: **Am I safe here?**

Safety, of course, includes clinical precision — accurate dosing, sterile procedures, and careful checks. But safety is broader than protocols. It's emotional. Patients often don't understand the intricacies of care, but they know instinctively whether they feel protected or exposed.

A nurse who explains each step before beginning, a physician who double-checks a medication, a technician who says, *"You're in good hands"* — these moments build a fortress of trust around the patient. Conversely, a rushed explanation, an unanswered question, or a visible mistake cracks that foundation instantly.

Patients may not always articulate safety in medical terms, but they carry the felt sense of it. And that sense often determines whether they relax enough to heal or remain locked in anxiety.

Safety isn't something assumed. It's something created, moment by moment — in the way care is explained, in the way concerns are taken seriously, in the way vigilance is shown. Without safety, nothing else sticks. With safety, almost anything is bearable.

"Encouragement reminds people that healing isn't only about what's broken. It's about what's strong in them, too."

#15 ENCOURAGEMENT AS MEDICINE

Encouragement is too often treated as optional — but patients describe it as transformative. Words like

"You're doing great" or "I'm proud of how far you've come"

may seem small, but to patients, they're fuel. Illness is exhausting. Recovery feels endless. Progress often comes in increments too small for patients to see themselves. Encouragement bridges that gap. It shines a light on progress when patients can't see it.

One man recalled how his therapist celebrated the fact that he could walk to the mailbox without pain.

"To me, it felt like nothing. But she said, 'That's a milestone.' That changed everything." Another said, "He told me my effort mattered. For the first time, I felt strong instead of broken."

Here's the why: recognition builds resilience. When patients feel their effort is noticed, their motivation increases. Encouragement turns compliance into confidence.

Encouragement isn't fluff. It's medicine. It reminds people that healing isn't only about what's broken — it's about what's strong in them, too.

"What happens in one room doesn't stay in one room. It ripples outward."

#16 THE RIPPLE EFFECT — PATIENT, TEAM, ORGANIZATION

A single moment of presence can transform a patient's trust. That trust spreads to their family, who retell the story:

"They cared for me like I mattered."

Those stories travel into communities, shaping reputations far more powerfully than billboards or marketing campaigns ever could.

The ripple moves inward too. Providers who connect deeply with patients often rediscover the joy of medicine. A single *"thank you"* from a grateful patient can sustain a physician through weeks of stress. Compassion, when mutual, becomes not just something given, but something replenished.

Teams feel it as well. A culture that prioritizes dignity, safety, and connection reduces burnout and strengthens collaboration. When staff feel supported and valued, they pass that on — first to each other, then to patients. The behind-the-scenes culture becomes the front-line experience.

I've seen this play out in real time. I worked with one organization where a single department started implementing intentional connection practices —

greeting patients by name, pausing before entering rooms, following up after difficult conversations. Within six months, their patient satisfaction scores rose. But what surprised leadership was that staff satisfaction rose too. The nurses said they felt like they were practicing medicine the way they'd always wanted to. Connection didn't just help patients. It healed the team.

And so, a single choice to pause, to listen, to connect does more than improve one patient's day. It strengthens trust in the team. It builds resilience in the provider. It shapes the reputation of the organization.

This is the hidden truth: what begins in one exam room can ripple outward until it transforms an entire system.

"Patients read the room before they meet your team. The space tells them what kind of care to expect."

#17
THE ROOM SPEAKS BEFORE YOU DO

Before a word is spoken, before a hand is extended, before a name is called — the building has already made its impression. Patients experience care with all of their senses, and the physical environment is shaping their trust before any human interaction begins.

I learned this by accident. Early in my work, I was visiting two clinics on the same day — both part of the same health system, both staffed by competent, caring teams. The first had harsh fluorescent lighting, a waiting room TV blaring cable news with a shooting on the screen, chairs packed so tightly that strangers were touching elbows, and a faint smell of cleaning chemicals. I watched patients sitting rigidly, arms crossed, eyes down. Nobody looked comfortable. Nobody looked like they wanted to be there — which, of course, they didn't. But the room was making it worse.

The second clinic, twenty minutes away, had warmer lighting, soft background music, space between the chairs, and a small sign near the door that read,

"We're glad you're here."

And then I saw it: patients settling in. Shoulders dropping.

A woman pulling out a book instead of gripping her phone. An older man chatting quietly with the person next to him. The people hadn't changed. The room had.

I started paying closer attention after that. I began noticing what patients noticed — the temperature, the cleanliness of the restroom, whether the magazines were from this decade, what was on the television, whether the signage helped or confused, whether the space felt like a warehouse or a place that had been thought about. And I started asking patients about it. Their answers surprised me in their specificity.

One woman told me,

"The waiting room told me everything I needed to know. If they can't even make this space feel decent, how much attention are they paying to the stuff I can't see?" A man said, "I noticed the bathroom was spotless. That sounds silly, but it made me think: if they care about this, they probably care about me."

Another patient described walking into a clinic that had replaced the standard waiting room TV with a screen displaying the provider's name, photo, and a message:

"Your provider is looking forward to seeing you today."

She told me it made her feel expected — like someone knew she was coming and was ready for her.

These details aren't cosmetic. They're psychological. Patients arrive already anxious — about the diagnosis, about the cost, about the vulnerability of being examined. Their nervous system is scanning for signals: Is this place safe? Am I going to be taken care of here? Does anyone even know I exist? The environment answers those questions before anyone on staff gets the chance to.

A chaotic, cluttered, harsh-lit space says: We're overwhelmed. You're one of many. Brace yourself. A calm, clean, intentionally designed space says: We thought about you before you got here.

This is also where the people who maintain those spaces — environmental services, facilities teams, office managers — become part of the care team, even if nobody has ever told them that. The housekeeper who keeps the restroom clean, the maintenance worker who replaces the flickering light in exam room three, the office manager who chose to turn off the waiting room TV — these people are shaping the patient's emotional state before a single clinical decision is made. They deserve to know their work matters to patients. Because it does.

I think about the environments I've walked through over the years — hundreds of clinics, hospitals, waiting rooms, hallways. The ones patients remember fondly almost never had the fanciest furniture or the newest paint. They had intention. Someone had thought about what it felt like to walk in scared and sit down. Someone had asked the question that too few organizations ask: If our building could talk, what would it tell patients about how much we care?

The answer to that question is worth sitting with. Because your patients already know.

"Healthcare was never just about treatments and diagnoses. At its core, it's about human connection."

#18
FROM PRINCIPLES TO PATIENT VOICES

We began by exploring what patients long for in their most vulnerable moments: dignity, presence, honesty, safety, hope, and partnership. We examined why these desires aren't extras, but essentials — rooted in human nature, intensified by fear and uncertainty, and remembered long after the clinical details fade.

Healthcare was never just about treatments and diagnoses. At its core, it's about human connection. Patients know this. They tell us this. The question is whether we have the courage to listen and act on what we already know.

Now, we turn to their voices. In the chapters ahead, patients themselves will tell us — clearly, directly, sometimes painfully — what makes them feel valued and what makes them feel invisible. They'll show us the gaps, but also the opportunities. They'll reveal, in their own words, the blueprint for care that heals not only bodies, but hearts and trust.

Part I has given us the why. Part II gives us the what.

The task before us is to listen.

PART II — TURNING PATIENT FEEDBACK INTO BETTER CARE

Now we hear from patients themselves — clearly, directly, sometimes painfully. These chapters follow the arc of the patient journey: from the first phone call, through the visit, into the hardest moments, and out the door into what comes after. Each chapter opens with a patient's or family member's voice, because this section belongs to them.

"I almost didn't come in. The parking lot almost won. But the woman at the front desk said, 'I'm glad you made it.' And I thought, okay. Maybe this will be different."
— Patient, 53

#1 BEFORE I EVEN SEE THE DOCTOR

"I called to make an appointment and the person who answered sounded annoyed — like I was interrupting their day. I almost hung up. When I finally got there, the check-in process felt cold. No eye contact. Just 'Name? Date of birth? Insurance card.' Like I was being processed through a system, not welcomed into a place that was supposed to help me.

By the time the doctor walked in, I was already tense. Already guarded. Already second guessing myself. And the thing is, the doctor was great. She was warm and thorough and kind. But I had to fight through forty minutes of feeling invisible just to be open with her.

I keep thinking — what if the front desk had smiled? What if someone had said, 'We're glad you're here'? I think I would've walked into that exam room a different person."

— Patient, 41

She told me later she almost canceled the appointment that morning.

"I sat in the parking lot for ten minutes deciding whether to go in. If the front desk had been different, I wouldn't have had to convince myself."

Patients start forming their opinion of your care before they ever see a provider. The front desk isn't the opening act — it is the first act.

I've spent years observing healthcare from the inside, and here's what I can tell you with certainty: patients don't separate the front desk from the doctor. In their mind, it's one experience. One organization. One feeling. The receptionist who doesn't look up, the phone system that puts them on hold for twelve minutes, the clipboard shoved across a counter — those moments don't disappear when the exam room door opens. They follow the patient in.

And yet, front desk staff are often the most under-trained, under-recognized, and under-supported people in the building.

They're handling insurance denials, running late schedules, managing frustrated patients, and answering phones — all at once, often without the tools or the authority to solve the problems landing in front of them. They're expected to be the face of the organization without being treated like they're part of the care team.

That needs to change. Because front desk staff don't just check patients in. They set the emotional temperature for the entire visit. A warm greeting, a moment of eye contact, a simple

"Thank you for coming in today"

— those ten seconds can lower a patient's anxiety before they ever reach the exam room.

And a cold, transactional check-in can raise it just as fast.

I once watched a receptionist completely transform a waiting room. An elderly man walked in looking confused and overwhelmed — clearly his first time at this clinic. Instead of pointing him toward the clipboard, she stood up, walked around the counter, and said,

"Let me help you with this. We're glad you're here."

She sat with him for two minutes helping him fill out the forms. Every other patient in that waiting room watched it happen. The whole energy shifted.

That's not a clinical skill. That's a human skill. And it changed the room.

The phone experience matters just as much. For many patients, the first interaction with your organization is a phone call — and it's often the worst. Long hold times, confusing menu trees, rushed schedulers who sound like they're reading a script. Patients tell me they judge the whole organization by that call.

"If they can't even answer the phone like they care, how are they going to care for me?"

Scheduling is another invisible pain point. When a patient calls in distress and the next available appointment is six weeks out, the way that message is delivered matters enormously.

"We don't have anything until March" feels like a door slamming. "The soonest I have is March 15th, but let me put you on our cancellation list so we can try to get you in sooner — and here's what to do if things get worse before then"

feels like someone is still holding the rope.

In practice:

- Train front desk staff as part of the care team, not separate from it. Include them in patient experience conversations, huddles, and recognition.
- Script the first ten seconds. Not robotically — but ensure every patient hears warmth in the first interaction: *"Welcome. We're glad you're here."*
- Redesign the phone experience. Mystery-call your own office. Time the hold. Listen to the tone. Ask yourself: would I come here?
- Empower front desk staff to solve problems. If they have to say *"I don't know" or "That's not my department"* ten times a day, the system is failing them — and failing patients.
- Acknowledge the wait at check-in. *"We're running about fifteen minutes behind. Can I get you anything while you wait?"* turns frustration into connection.

Reflection: If a patient never made it past the front desk, would they still feel cared for by your organization?

"I didn't dread going back because they made me feel like they were glad to see me."
— Patient, 72

#2 POSITIVITY — "I WANT TO FEEL WELCOMED."

"I usually walk into appointments guarded, but this one confirmed why. The tone was cold right away — no eye contact, quick questions, like they were trying to get through me as fast as possible. I could feel myself tense up even more. My shoulders stayed tight. My voice got weak.

I tried to explain what I was worried about, but it felt like I was interrupting. They kept typing. They didn't really look up. And the more rushed it felt, the more I started editing myself. I stopped asking questions because I didn't want to seem difficult or clueless.

I left with that awful feeling that I didn't say the most important thing. I didn't feel cared for. I felt managed. And honestly, I didn't want to go back."

— Patient, 38

She didn't go back. She found a new provider three months later — someone a friend recommended as

"the kind of doctor who actually looks at you."

She's been there for two years now and hasn't missed an appointment.

The tone of a visit is set long before the exam begins. Patients read the energy of a room before anyone says a word. They notice whether the space feels tense, rushed, or warm. They notice whether staff greet them with eye contact or glance past them.

Positivity isn't about forced cheer or pretending everything is perfect. It's about showing up with a presence that communicates: You are welcome here.

Think about walking into two different clinics. In the first, the receptionist doesn't look up, the nurse moves briskly, and the provider enters already distracted. In the second, you're greeted with a smile, thanked for waiting, and spoken to with genuine kindness. The medical care may be the same, but the experience is entirely different.

One patient said it plainly:

"I didn't dread going back because they made me feel like they were glad to see me."

When I walk into clinics, I can usually tell within thirty seconds whether the patients feel welcome. It's not the furniture or the paint colors. It's the front desk. It's whether the first human interaction a patient has makes them feel like a person or a number.

In practice: Positivity shows up in simple gestures — a smile on a hard day, a word of encouragement and gratitude for a patient's effort to follow through. Kindness is contagious.

When providers and staff radiate it, patients mirror it back, and the encounter becomes lighter for everyone.

Reflection: How does your presence make others feel when you walk into a room?

"I decided not to mention the other symptom because I didn't think he wanted to hear it."
— Patient, 56

#3 PATIENCE — "PLEASE DON'T RUSH MY STORY."

"She let me talk without cutting me off. That's rare."
— Patient, 44

Sometimes a patient's story says everything that needs to be said. I want to let this one stand on its own for a moment, because it captures something providers might not realize: how unusual it feels to a patient when someone simply lets them finish.

Time pressures in healthcare are real. But patients know when they're being hurried. And when they feel rushed, they edit themselves. They cut out details. Sometimes, they leave out the very information that matters most.

Patients tell us repeatedly: what they want is patience. Not unlimited time, but enough space to finish their story. Enough silence to let their words settle before the provider moves on.

One man said,

"I could tell he was ready to leave before I was done talking. I decided not to mention the other symptom because I didn't think he wanted to hear it."

That unmentioned symptom turned out to be the one that mattered most. He was diagnosed with a condition three months later - at a different practice - with a symptom he'd been too rushed to bring up previously.

Another patient contrasted that with a provider who leaned back, folded her hands, and said,

"Take your time. I want to hear the whole thing." "That," the patient said, "made me feel like I mattered."

Patience isn't about minutes. It's about respect. It communicates: You're worth listening to.

In practice: Resist the urge to interrupt. Allow silence. Give patients the sense that their full story is welcome, even when the schedule is tight.

Reflection: What important details might you be missing because you're moving too quickly?

"I stopped talking because I realized he wasn't really there. His body was. His attention wasn't."
— Patient, 33

#4 PRESENCE — "I WANT TO FEEL LIKE THE ONLY PERSON IN THE ROOM."

"I can tell within seconds if someone is actually with me. If they're typing the whole time, looking at the screen, checking the clock... I start talking less. I keep it surface-level. I just want to get out of the way.

But when someone sits down and looks at me — like I'm the only thing they're doing right then — I feel myself relax. I feel safe enough to say what I was scared to say."

— Patient, 50

Presence doesn't take more time. It takes more intention.

Presence is the currency of trust. For patients, nothing communicates care more powerfully than undivided attention. And yet, in modern healthcare, presence is often the hardest gift to give.

Patients know when you're with them and when you're somewhere else — still thinking about the last patient, glancing at the clock, typing as they talk. To them, these small actions don't read as *"busy." They read as "I'm not worth your time."*

One patient described how their provider sat down, leaned forward, and simply listened without interruption.

"I felt like I was the only person that mattered. It didn't take long, but it changed everything."

Contrast this with the patient who said,

"I stopped talking because I realized he wasn't really there. His body was. He attention wasn't."

The irony is that presence doesn't take more time. It takes intention. Even 90 seconds of pure focus can outweigh 15 distracted minutes. Patients rarely expect hours of undivided attention — they just want to feel that, for a moment, they matter more than the chart.

In practice: Stop looking at the computer. Turn toward the patient. Use intentional eye contact. Repeat back what they've said to show you heard them.

Reflection: Are you giving patients your presence, or just your time?

" One time, I even googled half of what they told me in the parking lot because I was too ashamed to admit I didn't get it."
— Patient, 43

#5 SPEAK MY LANGUAGE — "EXPLAIN THINGS SO I CAN UNDERSTAND."

"I've had appointments in the past where I left feeling stupid. There's no nicer way to say it. The doctor would explain things so quickly, using words I had never heard in my life, and I'd sit there nodding like I understood. Inside, I felt small. I felt embarrassed. I felt like asking a question would make me look even more clueless. So I stayed quiet.

One time, I even googled half of what they told me in the parking lot because I was too ashamed to admit I didn't get it. And the worst part was realizing later that I had misunderstood something important because I was too intimidated to speak up. That still bothers me.

But then I met a provider who did the exact opposite. They slowed down. They used words I actually understood. They didn't talk down to me, but they didn't talk over me either. They explained things like they genuinely wanted me to get it.

And for the first time in a long time, I felt smart instead of small. I felt like I was part of the conversation, not just being lectured. I felt respected. I wasn't afraid to ask questions. I wasn't afraid to say, 'Can you explain that again?'

That one experience changed everything for me. It made me realize how much the way someone talks to you shapes how you see yourself. It made me believe I could understand my own health, not just endure it." — ***Patient, 43***

That patient went on to become one of the most engaged people in her care team's practice. She asks questions at every visit now. She even helps other patients in the waiting room understand their paperwork. One conversation gave her permission to participate in her own health.

Plain language doesn't weaken your expertise. It honors the patient.

Medical jargon is like a locked door. Patients may nod politely, but often they walk away confused, intimidated, or even ashamed to admit they didn't understand. Complex language reinforces distance — the provider as expert, the patient as outsider.

But when providers translate information into everyday terms, the effect is immediate. Anxiety softens. Confidence grows. Patients shift from passive listeners to active participants in their care. It isn't about *"dumbing down"* medicine — it's about showing respect.

One provider described her turning point:

"I realized I was saying 'hypertension' while my patients just wanted me to say, 'high blood pressure.' They already felt overwhelmed. Why add another barrier?"

Plain language doesn't weaken your expertise. It honors the patient. It says: You belong in this conversation.

In practice: Providers who pause and say, *"Does that make sense?"* or *"Here's another way to put it"* invite clarity. Analogies, visuals, or even a quick drawing on scrap paper can make a diagnosis less frightening. Patients don't just want answers — they want understanding.

Reflection: When was the last time a patient left your care more confident because of how you explained something?

"It's not about being sensitive. It's about being treated like a human when you're already vulnerable."
— Patient, 57

#6 PROTECT MY DIGNITY — "SEE ME EVEN WHEN I'M VULNERABLE."

"I feel so uncomfortable being in a gown. I feel exposed and powerless right away. I know it's routine for them, but it doesn't feel routine when it's you.

I've had visits where I'm sitting there cold, trying to hold the gown closed, and people come in like I'm not even there. No knock. Curtain opens too fast. Someone starts talking to the computer or to the nurse instead of to me. And I'm just... on display. It makes your stomach drop.

Then everything feels rushed. Questions come rapid-fire, like there's a right answer and I'm behind. If I try to explain something, I can feel the impatience. And once I get the vibe that I'm slowing things down, I stop talking. I don't ask the question I meant to ask. I don't bring up the symptom I'm embarrassed about. I just nod and wait for it to be over.

Afterward, I don't leave thinking, 'That went fine.' I leave feeling small. Like I didn't have any control and I didn't deserve any space. And honestly, it makes it harder to come back.

It's not about being 'sensitive.' It's about being treated like a human when you're already vulnerable."

— Patient, 57

I followed up with this patient months later. She told me she'd started bringing a list of questions to appointments and handing it to her provider at the start:

"Here's what I need to talk about." It was her way of taking back some control. "I shouldn't have to do that," she said. "But until they slow down, it's how I protect myself."

Dignity is fragile but powerful. When you protect it, you build the trust that makes healing possible.

Healthcare strips away layers of identity. A teacher, a parent, a leader, a neighbor — suddenly reduced to

"the patient in room three."

Vulnerability can easily tip into humiliation if dignity is overlooked.

Patients remember moments when their dignity was either preserved or undermined. A nurse who pulled a curtain closed before asking a sensitive question. A provider who paused to explain each step of an exam before proceeding. A tech who draped a sheet carefully. These acts told the patient: You are still a person, not just a body.

On the other hand, patients recall with pain when dignity was disregarded.

"They talked about me like I wasn't there."
"The door was wide open."

These are small oversights that felt enormous.

Dignity is fragile, but it's also powerful. When you protect it, you build trust and confidence. When it's lost, it can sour the entire relationship.

In practice: Knock before entering. Use a patient's name. Explain procedures before they happen. Assume that every moment of vulnerability needs a shield of respect.

Reflection: If you were in their place, would you feel seen as a person or processed as a task?

"He cared about my faith as much as my symptoms. That's when I stopped holding back."
— Patient, 46

#7 RESPECT MY CULTURE — "UNDESRTAND WHERE I COME FROM."

"I was nervous to even bring it up because I've had people roll their eyes before. My beliefs are important to me, and I didn't want to be treated like I was being difficult or dramatic.

But she didn't laugh. She didn't make a face. She just asked about it — calmly, like it mattered. She said, 'Tell me what's important to you so we can make a plan that fits.' And I felt this huge wave of relief, like... okay, I can be myself here.

It wasn't just respectful. It made me feel safe. It made me trust her more, because she wasn't trying to squeeze me into some one-size-fits-all version of care. She made room for me.

That's the difference. I didn't feel judged. I felt understood."
— Patient, 24

That patient is now three years into a treatment plan that accounts for her faith practices. She hasn't missed a dose. She credits the relationship:

"I follow through because the plan was made for my actual life, not someone else's."

Culture isn't a nice-to-know. It's the lens through which patients experience everything you do.

Culture shapes how people experience illness, healing, family, and even silence. For some, prayer is part of treatment. For others, decisions can't be made without the family present. Culture isn't an optional layer — it's the lens through which everything about care gets interpreted.

Patients feel the difference when their culture is respected. One man described how his doctor asked about dietary restrictions tied to his faith before recommending treatment.

"He cared about my faith as much as my symptoms. That's when I stopped holding back."

Another patient shared how a nurse simply asked,

"What traditions are important to you as we plan your care?"

That simple question built trust.

Providers don't need to know everything about every culture. What matters is curiosity. Asking instead of assuming. Listening instead of labeling. Approaching each patient with humility.

When culture is dismissed, patients feel unseen — even unsafe. When it's honored, they feel welcome as they are.

In practice: Ask, *"Are there any traditions or values I should know about to better care for you?"* Make space for difference without judgment.

Reflection: What are you doing to grow your awareness of different cultures and beliefs you encounter?

"I didn't realize how guarded I was until he said, 'Yeah, I've dealt with that too.' It wasn't a big dramatic story.....it made me feel less alone."
— Patient, 63

#8 BE HUMAN TOO — "LET ME SEE WHO YOU ARE."

"I didn't realize how guarded I was until he said something like, 'Yeah, I've dealt with that too.' It wasn't a big dramatic story. It was just a human moment. And it made me feel less alone and less embarrassed about what I was dealing with. After that, I believed him more because it felt like he actually got it."

— Patient, 63

Three simple words — 'I believe you' — can end the loneliest fight a patient faces.

Professionalism has often been confused with distance — polished, composed, detached. But patients don't want a robot. They want a real person they can trust.

When a provider shares a small, appropriate piece of themselves — an honest acknowledgment, a relatable moment, even a quick laugh — it changes the tone of the room. It signals, I'm here with you. Patients consistently describe these moments as calming. They feel safer. They open up more. And the relationship feels more equal.

One patient remembered their doctor saying,

"My back went out once, too. I know how painful that can be."

It wasn't a long story. It was simply a moment of recognition. And it made the patient feel understood.

Showing your humanity doesn't weaken your credibility. It's what earns it. Authenticity strengthens rapport, and rapport strengthens trust. Patients don't just want expertise — they want to feel cared for by someone who sees them.

In practice: Share thoughtfully. A single sentence can be enough: *"That would be hard for me too," or "You're not alone in this."* Keep it brief, patient-centered, and in service of trust.

Reflection: What small piece of humanity could you offer that helps patients feel safe with you?

"When my doctor asked about my schedule before suggesting treatment, I felt like he saw me." — Patient, 51

#9 PERSONALIZE — "SEE ME, NOT JUST MY SYMPTOMS."

"I'm more than a diagnosis. I'm a whole person. But in that appointment, everything felt like a checklist. They didn't ask how it was affecting my life. They didn't ask what I was worried about. They just talked about my condition like I wasn't even in the room.

I left with instructions and pills, but I didn't leave feeling cared for. I left feeling like a problem they were trying to manage."

— Patient, 34

Personalization is what separates treating a condition from caring for a human being.

No two patients are the same, yet too often they feel treated like interchangeable cases. Personalization is what separates treating a condition from caring for a human being. It means seeing the individual behind the symptoms — their routine, responsibilities, fears, support system, and what "better" actually looks like in their real life.

Patients can feel it when care is copy-and-paste. They also feel it when a provider adjusts in small, meaningful ways: asking about work hours before recommending a plan, checking what support they have at home, or asking what they're most worried about before launching into options. One patient said,

"When my doctor asked about my schedule before suggesting treatment, I felt like he saw me."

Another recalled,

"She asked what mattered most to me, not just what would fix my numbers. That changed everything."

Personalization doesn't mean ignoring evidence or bending medicine to preference. It means practicing good medicine in context. When care connects to a patient's actual life, patients understand it better, follow through more consistently, and trust more deeply — because the plan feels realistic, not theoretical.

In practice: Use their name. Reference one continuity detail from a prior visit. Ask one life-anchoring question: *"What does a good day look like for you?"* or *"What's the hardest part of this in your normal routine?"* Then shape the plan so it fits their reality.

Reflection: If you had to describe your patient as a person — not a diagnosis — what would you say?

"When she asked how I was doing emotionally, I almost cried."
— Patient, 42

#10 **POUR IN** — "PLEASE TREAT ME LIKE A HUMAN."

"When she asked how I was doing emotionally, I almost cried. Not because anything dramatic happened in that moment — just because nobody ever asks that. I'm used to them asking about pain levels and symptoms, but not how I'm actually holding up. It made me feel like a person, not just a problem to fix."

— Patient, 42

When patients feel truly seen, they stop watching from the sidelines and start owning their care.

Every patient is carrying more than symptoms. They're carrying worry, pressure, uncertainty, and often the exhausting job of pretending they're fine. But healthcare has a way of narrowing people down to numbers, diagnoses, and next steps. Patients feel that shift immediately. When the visit becomes purely transactional, they start to edit themselves. They share less. They comply less. They leave feeling alone in it.

That's why small moments of humanity land so hard. A simple emotional check-in

— *"How are you holding up?"*

— Can feel almost shocking to a patient who's never been asked. Not because it's dramatic, but because it signals something rare: I see you. And when people feel truly seen, they stop watching from the sidelines and start owning their care.

Pouring in doesn't mean turning the exam room into therapy. It means bringing warmth to the clinical work. Tone matters. Pace matters. A pause matters. Sometimes the most effective care in the room is a ten-second acknowledgement:

"That sounds really hard."
"You're not overreacting."
"I'm glad you told me."

Providers worry this will take too long. In reality, it often saves time and lives — because patients stop performing and start telling the truth.

In practice: Ask one human question early (*"How are you holding up?"*). Pause long enough to let them answer. Name what you hear (*"That sounds heavy"*). Then connect it to the plan *("Knowing that helps me take better care of you.")*

Reflection: Do patients leave your room feeling managed — or genuinely seen?

"If she hadn't asked again, I don't think I'd be here."
— Patient, 35

#11 **PRESS IN —** "I NEED YOU TO ASK THE HARD QUESTIONS."

"I told him I was fine. I even smiled and laughed when I said it. That's what I do — I don't want to be a burden.

But he didn't just accept it and move on. He paused and said, 'Okay… but I'm going to ask again. Are you really okay?' And something about the way he said it — calm, not judging, not rushing — made it harder to hide behind the same answer.

The first time I said 'fine' out of habit. The second time, I felt like he actually wanted the truth.

I didn't spill everything at once, but I finally admitted I wasn't doing well. And honestly, I don't know what would've happened if he hadn't asked again. That second question mattered more than he'll probably ever realize."

— Patient, 47

He's in treatment now. He told me later,

"That appointment probably saved my life. Not the medicine — the question."

When people feel safe enough, the truth finally comes out.

Patients don't always say what hurts most. Sometimes they minimize their pain.

Sometimes shame or fear keeps them silent. Sometimes they've been dismissed before and don't want to risk it again. And sometimes they simply forget — because stress makes it hard to organize thoughts, remember symptoms, or explain what's been happening. That's why *"I'm fine"* can mean the opposite, and why thoughtful questions can surface what a patient didn't know how to say — or didn't remember to say — until you asked.

Pressing in doesn't mean pushing. It means gently creating space for honesty. It means asking the second question. It means waiting in the silence long enough for truth to surface.

One patient shared how their provider leaned in and said,

"I know you said you're okay. But can I ask again — are you really?"

That small insistence opened the door to a conversation that revealed depression and thoughts of self-harm. The patient later said,

"If she hadn't asked again, I don't think I'd be here."

When patients feel safe, they disclose more. But safety often comes only after persistence. The willingness to ask the uncomfortable question, to stay present in the hard silence, is sometimes the difference between healing and harm.

In practice: Don't stop at the first answer. Ask open-ended questions. If intuition tells you there's more, lean in with gentleness.

Reflection: What questions are you not asking that might change the story?

"I was so tired of making my case. I just wanted someone to stop questioning and start helping."
— Patient, 48

#12 FEEL MY PAIN — "ACKNOWLEDGE WHAT I'M GOING THROUGH."

"When the scans didn't show anything, the whole tone changed. They got dismissive, like the problem was me. I left feeling ashamed and frustrated — still in pain, but now also feeling like I wasn't taken seriously. It made me feel hopeless."
— Patient, 52

"When someone finally feels believed, the exhausting fight to be taken seriously stops — and the real work can begin."

Pain isn't just physical. It comes with fear, frustration, exhaustion, and sometimes a long history of not being taken seriously. When patients feel doubted, dismissed, or brushed off, the pain gets heavier — not because it changes in the body, but because they're carrying it alone.

A lot of people with chronic or hard-to-measure pain learn to come prepared like they're making a case. They track symptoms, rehearse what to say, and still worry they'll be labeled dramatic or anxious. When a provider says, *"I believe you,"* it can bring immediate relief. Not because the pain disappears, but because the exhausting fight to be taken seriously finally stops.

Validation doesn't replace diagnosis or treatment. It sets the tone for both.

Acknowledging suffering

— *"That sounds really hard," "I can see how much this is affecting you," "I believe you"* —

reduces distress and builds trust. It turns the visit from interrogation into partnership.

Providers can't always remove pain. But they can always acknowledge it. And for many patients, that acknowledgment is what they remember most.

In practice: Start with belief and curiosity. Ask how pain impacts daily life (*"What does this keep you from doing?"*). Name what you're hearing. Explain next steps clearly, especially when tests are inconclusive.

Reflection: When pain is invisible, do your words make patients feel doubted — or supported?

"They danced around it for weeks. When I finally found out, I wasn't just scared. I was angry they'd waited."
— Patient, 59

#13 **KEEP IT HONEST** — "TELL ME THE TRUTH, EVEN WHEN IT'S HARD."

"She didn't sugarcoat it, but she said it with kindness."
— Patient, 26

Patients don't need you to soften reality. They need the truth delivered with compassion.

Honesty is one of the clearest forms of respect a provider can offer. Patients don't need false reassurance, and they don't want to be managed with vague language. They want the truth — because it's their body, their life, their decisions. But they need that truth delivered in a way that doesn't leave them feeling flattened or alone.

Patients can feel the difference between clarity and avoidance. When providers *"dance around it,"* patients start to sense something is being withheld. They go home and spiral. Search online. They reread portal results. They wonder what they're not being told. And when the truth finally comes out, it doesn't just land as hard news — it lands as a loss of trust.

The best honesty is direct and steady. It doesn't dramatize. It doesn't rush. It makes space for reaction. It pairs reality with support: *"This is serious." "Here's what that means." "Here's what we do next."*

That combination — truth plus presence — is what turns fear into partnership.

Honesty doesn't remove hope. It grounds it. It gives patients agency to prepare, plan, ask questions, and make choices. Even when the answer is difficult, clarity creates stability. Silence creates panic.

In practice: Use plain language. Don't delay the message. Say what you know and what you don't. Pause, then check understanding. Close with a clear next step and a support statement patients can hold onto: *"We'll take this one step at a time, and I'll stay with you through it."*

Reflection: When the news is hard, do your patients leave with clarity — or with confusion?

"She asked, 'What would make this hard to follow?' Nobody had ever asked me that. It changed the whole plan."
— Patient, 44

#14 PARTNERSHIP — "I WANT TO BE PART OF THE PLAN."

"One time during an appointment the plan was basically decided before I opened my mouth. They told me what to do, handed me instructions, and that was it. I didn't feel comfortable pushing back, even when I knew parts of it wouldn't work for my life. So I nodded, left, and then... didn't follow through the way I should have. Not because I didn't care — because it didn't feel like it was made for me.

What I want is simple. Ask me what matters to me. Ask what I'm worried about. Ask what I can realistically do. I don't need to run the medical side, but I do need to be part of the decision — because I'm the one who has to live with it after I leave the room."

— Patient, 39

Patients don't just want a plan that's medically right. They want one they can actually live with.

For a long time, medicine trained patients to be passive. Follow instructions. Don't interrupt. Don't question. But patients today want something more practical and more respectful: collaboration. They want a plan that's medically right and that they can actually live with.

When patients don't feel included, they tend to disengage. They might agree in the room and quietly opt out later. They might skip medications, avoid follow-ups, or *"forget"* the plan — not out of apathy, but because the plan never felt like theirs. Partnership closes that gap. It turns compliance into commitment, because the patient has ownership.

Partnership doesn't mean abandoning expertise. It means combining clinical knowledge with lived reality. A provider brings evidence and experience. The patient brings context: work schedule, family responsibilities, fears, values, support, barriers, goals. When those are brought into the conversation early, the plan gets smarter — and follow-through gets stronger.

The shift can be small but powerful. Instead of

"Here's what we're going to do," it becomes *"Here are the options. Here's what I recommend and why. Now tell me what matters most to you, and what feels realistic."*

That tone change creates trust. It also surfaces the things that derail care if they stay hidden — cost, transportation, side effects, shame, confusion, overwhelm.

In practice: Offer options when you can. Ask, *"What matters most to you right now?"* and *"What would make this hard to follow?"* Confirm alignment before closing: *"Here's what we decided together — does that feel doable?"*

Reflection: In your care, are patients agreeing in the room — and opting out later? Or are you building plans they can actually own?

"She opened with, 'Here's what I know so far.' I thought, finally — someone did the homework."
— Patient, 45

#15 PREPARED — "I WANT YOU TO KNOW WHO I AM."

"When I scheduled my appointment, my doctor reached out and told me to get labs done ahead of time, so the visit would be more productive. I did them two days before, got the results in my portal, and walked in thinking, Okay, at least we'll be able to talk through this.

But during the appointment, after I explained what I was dealing with, he started talking about ordering labs — like we hadn't already done them. I asked, 'Are these different from the ones I just did?' and he said no.

It was such a gut-punch. Not because the labs were the issue, but because it made me realize he hadn't looked at my chart at all. I left feeling annoyed and honestly a little unsettled — like if I wasn't paying attention, we'd just repeat things and waste time. I don't want to feel like I have to quarterback my own care."

— Patient, 51

Preparation communicates respect. When a provider walks in knowing the patient's history, goals, and what happened last time, it tells them they matter enough for you to be ready. And when a provider isn't prepared, patients feel it immediately. It doesn't just create confusion — it creates doubt.

Patients can handle complexity. What they struggle with is inconsistency. Having to repeat themselves, correct the plan, or remind a clinician what was already decided makes them feel like the burden of coordination is on them. It turns the visit into work. It chips away at trust.

The difference is often simple. A prepared provider has read the chart, reviewed prior decisions, and connected the dots before walking in. They start the visit with continuity: Here's what we did last time. Here's what your labs showed. Here's what we're deciding today.

That one shift changes the entire experience. Patients relax. They ask better questions. They feel like a person with a story — not a case that resets every visit.

Being prepared isn't just clinical. It's relational. It's knowing the numbers and remembering what matters to the person sitting in front of you — what they're hoping for, what they're afraid of, what success looks like in their life.

In practice: Take 60 seconds before entering to review the last plan, the current results, and the patient's stated goals. Start by summarizing what you know and inviting correction: *"Here's what I'm tracking — what did I miss?"*

Reflection: When you walk in, does the patient feel like you're meeting them — or meeting the schedule?

"I sat in my car after the appointment thinking, 'Now what?' Nobody told me the next step."
— Patient, 73

#16 GUIDE ME THROUGH — "HELP ME NAVIGATE THIS SYSTEM."

"I've left appointments before with a diagnosis and a stack of papers, and then I just sat in my car like... okay, now what? I didn't know if I was supposed to call someone, wait for a call, schedule something, or deal with insurance first. It felt like I was on my own the second I walked out.

This time, they slowed down and walked me through it. They wrote it down in plain language. They told me what was next, what could wait, and who to contact if I got stuck. I left feeling calmer, like I wasn't going to mess it up."

— Patient, 73

A diagnosis without a next step feels like being dropped in the middle of nowhere.

For patients, healthcare can feel like a maze. Referrals, scheduling, portals, insurance approvals, billing — what's routine to a provider can be confusing and stressful when you're living it for the first time. And when people are scared or in pain, even *"simple"* instructions don't always stick. Patients don't just need information. They need clarity and direction.

A diagnosis without a next step can feel like being dropped in the middle of the process. Patients leave unsure who to call, what to schedule, what's urgent, and what can wait. That uncertainty doesn't just create frustration — it creates fear. On the other hand, a few minutes of guidance can completely change the experience: a quick overview of the plan, a written checklist, a name to contact, and a realistic timeline. That's often what patients mean when they say they felt cared for.

Guidance builds confidence. It reduces avoidable delays. It helps patients follow through. Most importantly, it tells them they're not alone in figuring it out.

In practice: Give a simple next-step roadmap. Write it down. Confirm understanding (*"What are you going to do when you leave here?"*). Share who to contact if they get stuck, and set expectations on timing.

Reflection: Are you handing patients instructions — or helping them leave with a plan they can actually follow?

"He said, 'This isn't forever.' Three words. But I held onto them for months."

— Patient, 41

#17 **GIVE ME HOPE** — "HELP ME BELIEVE THINGS CAN GET BETTER."

"Her encouragement made me believe I could heal."
— Patient, 58

Patients aren't asking for promises. They're just asking to see a path forward.

Hope isn't naïve. It's stabilizing. When patients are scared, exhausted, or stuck in a long stretch of symptoms, they don't just want information — they want a reason to believe the effort is worth it. They want to feel like improvement is possible, even if it's slow and uneven.

A lot of patients aren't asking for guarantees. They know you can't promise outcomes. What they're asking for is orientation. Is there a path? Have you seen people get better? Does my progress count, even if it's small? When providers never speak to the future, patients start to assume the future is bleak.

Hope doesn't come from hype. It comes from honesty paired with possibility. It sounds like, *"This is hard, and we're not ignoring that."* It sounds like, *"Here's what we can try next."*

It sounds like,

"You've already made progress, even if it doesn't feel dramatic."

It gives patients something to hold onto between visits — especially on the days they're tempted to give up.

The most credible hope is specific. It's tied to small wins, realistic timelines, and a plan. Sometimes it's a simple sentence that lands at the right time:

"You're doing better than you think."
"Your effort is showing."
"This isn't forever."

Those words don't change the diagnosis, but they can change the patient's ability to keep going.

In practice: Use future-focused language without overpromising. Name progress out loud. Break the path into manageable steps. When appropriate, share a realistic example of improvement: *"I've seen patients move through this, and we'll take it one step at a time."*

Reflection: Do your words leave patients bracing — or believing?

"She told me she was proud of me, and I realized I hadn't heard that in years."
— Patient, 33

#18 PRAISE — "ENCOURAGEMENT HELPS ME HEAL."

"She pointed out progress I was too tired to see. That's what kept me going."
— Patient, 54

So much of what patients do to get better never shows up on any scan.

Encouragement can sound small, but to patients it's often the difference between continuing and quietly quitting. Most progress in healthcare is invisible. It's the patient taking meds consistently when they don't feel like it. It's showing up even after a setback. It's making one better choice at lunch. It's doing the exercises again. It's calling to reschedule instead of disappearing. So much of what patients do to get better never shows up on any scan — and they're usually doing it while scared, tired, and doubting themselves.

That's why acknowledgment matters. When a provider names effort out loud, it validates the reality of what the patient is carrying. It also reduces shame. So many patients assume they're *"behind," "not doing it right," or "being difficult."*

A simple, specific statement

— *"You've been consistent,"*
"You're doing the hard part,"
"I can see the effort you're putting in" —

helps patients reframe their story from failure to forward motion.

Encouragement also creates clarity. Patients often don't know what *"good"* looks like. They don't know if side effects are normal. They don't know if slow improvement still counts. A provider can communicate expectations in a way that makes the path feel survivable:

"This is supposed to be gradual."
"Two steps forward and one back is still progress."
"The fact that you're here today tells me you haven't given up."

Patients aren't asking for cheerleading. They're asking for a signal that their effort is seen and that it matters. One patient said,

"She told me she was proud of me, and I realized I hadn't heard that in years."

Another described a clinician who celebrated small wins:

"She pointed out progress I was too tired to see."

That kind of reinforcement doesn't soften professionalism — it strengthens engagement. It turns a care plan into something a patient can stay with when motivation dips.

In practice:

- Be specific, not generic. *"You're doing great"* is nice. *"You kept your appointments even when this has been draining"* is powerful.
- Recognize effort and outcomes. *"Your numbers improved"* + *"Your consistency is what got you here."*
- Normalize setbacks. *"A rough week doesn't erase the work you've done."*
- Celebrate the behavior you want repeated. *"I'm glad you came back in — that's a strong move."*
- End with a forward step. *"Here's what we're building on next."*

Reflection: Do your patients leave feeling measured — or strengthened? When they walk out, do they feel like they're failing a test, or like they're making progress with a team behind them?

"She said, 'I'm going to check on you Friday.' And she did. That's when I knew she meant it."

— Patient, 47

#19 WALK WITH ME — "DON'T DISAPPEAR AFTER THE DIAGNOSIS."

"I've gotten bad news before and it felt like the room shut down right after. They told me, handed me a pamphlet, and stood up like the conversation was over. I was still sitting there trying to process it, and I could tell they were already mentally gone.

I walked out confused, shaky, and embarrassed for being emotional. I didn't even know what I was supposed to do next. I just remember thinking, So now I'm on my own with this?"

— Patient, 63

Walking with someone means staying long enough for the hard news to land — and then not leaving.

For many patients, the hardest moment isn't hearing the diagnosis — it's what happens right after. Too often, difficult news is delivered and then the room goes cold. The provider stands up. Papers appear. The visit moves on. And the patient is left sitting there, still trying to process what they just heard.

Patients describe it as a kind of quiet abandonment. Not always intentional, but real. A diagnosis gets handed over like information, not like a life moment.

And when someone is overwhelmed, they can't always form the right questions in the moment. They nod. They try to stay composed. Then they get to the car and it hits them — and they realize they don't know what's next, who to call, or how to hold the fear they're carrying.

Walking with patients doesn't mean solving everything. It means not vanishing. It means slowing down after the hardest words, staying present long enough for the news to land, and offering a path forward in plain language. It means making sure they leave with something steady: the next step, a timeline, a point of contact, and the reassurance that they're not being dropped into this alone.

Patients remember who stayed with them when the path got hard. And they remember who made them feel like the conversation was over the second the diagnosis was said.

In practice: Don't end the visit at the diagnosis. End it with a plan. Write down next steps, name who will follow up and when, and schedule the next touchpoint before they leave. A simple line like *"I'm going to check in"* matters — especially when you follow through.

Reflection: After hard news, do your patients feel handed off — or held up?

"We didn't make a fully informed decision. We made a pressured decision in a fog."
— Family Member

#20 CLARIFY MY CHOICES — "MAKE SURE I UNDESTAND BEFORE I SIGN."

"They asked about a DNR like it was just another box to check.

My loved one was struggling to breathe after a life saving treatment. We were exhausted, scared, and running out of options. The conversation kept circling the same things — steroids, opioids, comfort measures — like there wasn't much else to offer. And then someone brought up a DNR.

The way it was explained sounded like one thing: no life support. That's what he wanted. He didn't want machines keeping him alive forever. So he signed it.

But nobody stopped to make sure he understood what a DNR actually means. Nobody sat down and said, plainly, 'This means we won't do compressions. We won't put in a breathing tube if you stop breathing. We won't attempt resuscitation.' Nobody asked him to say it back in his own words. Nobody checked whether he meant, 'No long-term life support,' instead of 'Do not attempt to save my life if I crash.'

The worst part was the timing. The consult we were told we'd get didn't happen until the next day. So we sat in that gap — overnight — knowing something had been signed, but not truly knowing what it meant, while different parts of the hospital seemed to be operating on different assumptions.

When the consultation finally happened, he reversed it. He didn't want 'do not resuscitate.' He wanted 'no prolonged life support.' Those are not the same. And we almost learned that the hardest way possible.

That's what still haunts me: we didn't make a fully informed decision. We made a pressured decision in a fog."

— Family Member

He's still alive. The reversal happened in time. But the family told me they still think about that overnight gap — the hours when the wrong decision was on the chart.

"We got lucky," the family member said. "Not everyone does."

There are moments in healthcare where the language is deceptively simple, but the implications are enormous. Code status conversations are one of them. A few letters — DNR — can change the entire trajectory of care, not because anyone is being cruel, but because the system moves fast and the words get compressed.

This isn't about blame. It's about risk management through clarity.

When families are under stress, the brain doesn't process nuance the same way. They hear

"DNR" and translate it into *"don't keep me alive on machines."*

That may be exactly what the patient believes they're choosing. But in many environments, *"DNR"* is interpreted operationally as *"no CPR / no resuscitation,"* and that gap can become a safety event.

What patients and families need in these moments isn't more paperwork. They need translation, time anchoring, and decision confidence — the feeling that the choice was understood, aligned, and documented in a way the entire care team will execute consistently.

In practice:

- Slow the moment down. Treat code status like a *"high-stakes decision point,"* not an administrative checkbox.
- Use plain-language definitions. Avoid euphemisms. Speak directly and gently: what will happen, and what will not.
- Teach-back, without shame. *"I want to make sure I explained it clearly — can you tell me what this means in your own words?"*
- Separate *"no prolonged life support" from "do not resuscitate."* If your system supports nuanced orders (POLST/MOLST, limited interventions, time-limited trials), surface them explicitly rather than forcing binary choices.
- Create a one-page summary. What was decided, why, and what the patient values most — so the plan travels across shifts and units.

Reflection: When patients sign something that can change whether you attempt to save their life, does your process optimize for speed — or for understanding?

"Nobody said, 'We made an error and here's what happened."
— Patient, 28

#21 WHEN WE GET IT WRONG — "OWN IT. THAT'S ALL I ASK."

"The mistake wasn't what broke my trust. The silence afterward is what broke it.

Something went wrong during my procedure — I won't go into details, but it resulted in an extra week of recovery and a lot of pain I wasn't supposed to have. When I tried to ask about it, I got vague answers. 'Complications happen.' 'It's within the range of normal outcomes.' Nobody said, 'We made an error and here's what happened.'

I found out what actually went wrong months later, from a different doctor. And the thing is — I probably would have forgiven the mistake. People are human. But the cover-up? The deflection? That I can't forgive. Because it told me something about who they are when things get hard. And it's not who I want taking care of me."

— Patient, 58

He switched providers. He told me he didn't sue, but he considered it — not because of the complication, but because of the dishonesty.

"If someone had just said, 'I'm sorry, here's what happened, here's how we're going to make it right,' I'd probably still be their patient."

Patients don't expect perfect care. They expect honest care — especially when something goes wrong.

This is the chapter nobody wants to write, and nobody wants to need. But it might be the most important one in this book, because how an organization handles a mistake reveals more about its character than a thousand perfect visits ever could.

Mistakes happen in healthcare. Errors, miscommunications, dropped balls, bad days, system failures, human failures. Patients know this. They don't walk in expecting perfection. But they do walk in expecting honesty. And when something goes wrong — when a medication error occurs, when a diagnosis is missed, when communication breaks down, when a patient is treated poorly — what happens in the next sixty minutes will determine whether that patient stays or leaves, trusts or sues, forgives or tells everyone they know.

The instinct in healthcare is often to minimize, deflect, or go silent. Legal departments coach caution. Providers worry about liability. And so the patient — who is already hurt, confused, or scared — gets met with vagueness.

"Complications are not uncommon."
"We followed standard protocols."
"I'll look into it."

Those responses aren't reassurance. They're abandonment in professional clothing. What patients want after a mistake is remarkably simple: honesty, accountability, empathy, and a plan. *"Here's what happened. I'm sorry. Here's what we're doing about it. And here's how we're going to take care of you going forward."*

That combination doesn't increase liability — research consistently shows it decreases it. Patients sue when they feel abandoned or deceived. They rarely sue when they feel cared for, even after a bad outcome.

This principle extends beyond medical errors. It applies to every service failure in the building — the rude front desk interaction, the appointment that ran an hour late with no apology, the test result that was lost, the billing mistake that caused financial harm. Every one of these is a trust injury. And every one of them is an opportunity to repair trust through honest acknowledgment.

I've seen organizations that train for this — that practice service recovery as deliberately as they practice clinical skills. They empower every staff member, from the CEO to the housekeeper, to say three words that change everything: *"I am sorry."* Not *"I'm sorry you feel that way."* Not *"I'm sorry if there was a misunderstanding."* But a genuine, specific apology that names what went wrong and takes responsibility.

In practice:

- Create a service recovery framework that every team member can use. A simple model: Acknowledge, Apologize, Act, Follow up.
- Train providers and staff to apologize without deflection. *"I'm sorry this happened"* is not an admission of negligence. It's an act of humanity.
- Respond quickly. The longer the silence after a mistake, the louder it becomes in the patient's mind.

- Follow up after a service failure. A call from a manager or provider that says, *"I wanted to check in on how you're doing after what happened"* communicates care beyond the event itself.
- Separate service recovery from legal strategy. Patients can tell when they're being managed versus cared for. The instinct to protect the organization often harms it more.

Reflection: When something goes wrong in your organization, does the patient hear honesty first — or silence?

"The nurse turned to my daughter and said, 'What questions do you have?' We both exhaled."
— Family Member

#22 INCLUDE MY PEOPLE — "TALK TO MY FAMILY TOO."

"They talked to my wife like she mattered. That earned my trust."

— Patient, 66

Including loved ones doesn't push the patient aside. It widens the circle of people who care.

Patients rarely walk into care alone. Even when they show up by themselves, there's usually someone behind the scenes — spouses, adult children, friends, caregivers — helping them remember details, manage medications, ask the questions they forget, and hold things together when the situation is heavy. When providers acknowledge that support system, it doesn't dilute care. It strengthens it.

A lot of families don't want to take over the visit. They just want to be included in a way that makes the patient safer. Sometimes the spouse is the one who notices patterns the patient has normalized. Sometimes an adult child is the one tracking appointments and insurance. Sometimes the caregiver is the reason the plan actually happens after the visit ends. When those people are ignored, patients feel like the system is pretending they don't exist.

When they're included, patients feel supported instead of alone.

One patient described the moment it clicked for them: the provider didn't just tolerate their spouse being there — the provider turned and said, *"What questions do you have?"* Another family remembered a nurse who took time to explain next steps directly, not in a rushed way, but like the role of the caregiver was legitimate and respected. That kind of inclusion calms the whole room. It lowers anxiety. It reduces miscommunication. And it builds trust because it signals you're thinking beyond the appointment.

Including loved ones doesn't mean pushing the patient aside. It means widening the circle of care — while still keeping the patient at the center. With permission, it creates alignment: everyone leaves with the same understanding of the plan, the same expectations, and fewer gaps for fear or confusion to fill.

In practice: Ask early, *"Who do you want involved in this conversation?"* With permission, speak directly to family or caregivers. Invite their questions. Confirm the plan out loud so everyone hears it the same way, then summarize next steps in writing.

Reflection: Do your patients feel like they're carrying this alone — or like you're supporting the people who support them?

"I'm the one keeping all of this together. And I'm falling apart. Just once, I wanted someone to turn to me and say, 'How are you doing?.''
— Family member

#23 THE CAREGIVER IS A PATIENT TOO — "ASK HOW ARE YOU HOLDING UP?"

"Nobody checks on me. I'm here every day. I sleep in this chair. I manage his medications. I translate what the doctors say into words he understand. I call the insurance company. I argue with billing. I update the family group text every night. I haven't eaten a real meal in four days. I haven't showered since Tuesday.

And every time someone walks in, they look past me to him. Which I get — he's the patient. But I'm the one keeping all of this together. And I'm falling apart. Just once, I wanted someone to turn to me and say, 'How are you doing?' Not about him. About me."

— Family Caregiver, Wife of Patient, 62

She told me she finally broke down in the hospital cafeteria at 2 a.m. A janitor — not a nurse, not a doctor, a janitor — stopped and asked if she was okay. She said it was the first time in nine days anyone had asked her that. *"He sat with me for five minutes. I will never forget that man."*

Behind every patient, there's usually someone holding everything together. They're exhausted too. And they almost never get asked.

This book is about patients. But there's someone standing behind nearly every patient in this book — the caregiver. The spouse who sleeps in a recliner for a week. The adult daughter who drives three hours every other day. The friend who sits through chemo because nobody should do that alone. The parent who hasn't left the pediatric ICU since admission.

Caregivers aren't visitors. They're unpaid members of the care team. They manage medications, track symptoms, interpret medical language, coordinate schedules, handle insurance, update family, make decisions when the patient can't, and absorb the emotional weight of watching someone they love suffer. And they do all of it while running on no sleep, bad food, and fear.

And yet, the healthcare system treats them as background. They're

"the wife in the corner," or *"the daughter who keeps asking questions."*

They're tolerated, sometimes included, rarely cared for. Providers: the caregiver's well-being directly affects the patient's outcome. A caregiver who's exhausted makes more mistakes with medications. A caregiver who's uninformed can't follow the discharge plan. A caregiver who feels invisible stops advocating — and the patient loses their strongest ally.

I've watched a chaplain sit with a caregiver for ten minutes while the patient slept and simply say,

"Tell me how you're doing — not about your husband, about you."

The caregiver sobbed. She said she'd been holding it in for a week because she didn't think she was allowed to be the one who was struggling. That ten-minute conversation didn't cost the hospital anything. But it probably prevented a caregiver collapse that would have affected the patient's entire recovery.

In practice:

- Ask the caregiver one direct question: *"How are you holding up?"* Not about the patient. About them.
- Provide practical support: where to get food, where to shower, where to rest. Many caregivers don't know these resources exist.
- Include them in the plan — and make sure they understand it. They're the ones who'll execute it after discharge.
- Watch for caregiver burnout: weight loss, sleep deprivation, emotional flatness, withdrawal. They won't ask for help. You have to notice.
- Acknowledge their role. *"You're doing a really important job here. Your husband is lucky to have you."* That sentence costs nothing and means everything.

Reflection: When you walk into a patient's room and someone else is sitting there — exhausted, quiet, holding it together — do you see a visitor, or do you see someone who needs care too?

"I didn't understand half of what was on the discharge sheet. I just knew I was leaving, and I wasn't ready."

— Patient, 68

#24 THE GOODBYE MATTERS TOO — "DON'T RUSH THE EXIT."

"The discharge felt like being pushed out the door. Someone came in, read from a paper, asked me to sign something, and said I could get dressed. That was it. I didn't understand half of what was on the discharge sheet. I didn't know what medications I was supposed to stop or start. I didn't know when I should worry versus when I should wait. I just knew I was leaving, and I wasn't ready.

I sat in the wheelchair at the exit and thought, I don't feel safe going home. But I didn't say anything because everyone seemed busy and I didn't want to be difficult."

— Patient, 68

She was readmitted eleven days later. She told me,

"If someone had spent five more minutes with me before I left, I think I would have been okay. I just didn't understand the plan well enough to follow it."

The last five minutes of a hospital stay can determine whether a patient heals at home — or comes back.

In healthcare, discharge is often treated as an administrative event — paperwork to complete, a bed to free up, a process to close out.

But for patients, discharge is one of the most vulnerable moments in their care journey. They're leaving the safety of a building full of people who know what to do if something goes wrong, and they're going home to a kitchen table and a stack of confusing papers.

The way you send someone home is the last impression they carry. And it sets the tone for everything that happens next — whether they take the right medications, whether they watch for the right warning signs, whether they follow up on time, and whether they come back to your organization or go somewhere else.

I've seen discharges that took forty-five seconds. A nurse reads off a printed sheet, hands it to the patient, and says, *"Any questions?"* The patient — overwhelmed, medicated, exhausted — says no. And everyone moves on. That's not education. That's a liability exercise disguised as care.

I've also seen discharges that changed outcomes. A nurse sat on the edge of the bed, went through the plan slowly, used teach-back to confirm understanding, wrote the three most important things on an index card, and said,

"Call this number if anything feels off. Don't wait. Don't search online. Call us." That patient told me, *"I left feeling like I had a team behind me, even at home."*

The research is clear: poor discharge communication is one of the leading drivers of avoidable readmissions. But beyond the numbers, it's a trust issue.

A patient who leaves confused doesn't just face medical risk. They face the emotional weight of feeling abandoned at the moment they need support most.

In practice:

- Slow down the discharge. It's a care moment, not a clerical one. Sit down. Make eye contact. Talk like it matters — because it does.
- Use teach-back for the critical points. *"Tell me what you're going to do when you get home."* If they can't, you haven't finished.
- Write the three most important things on a card. Not the full discharge packet — just the three things that matter most in plain language: what to take, what to watch for, and who to call.
- Include the caregiver. They're the ones who'll be managing the plan. Make sure they heard it too.
- Schedule the follow-up before they leave. *"Your next appointment is Thursday at 10. You'll see Dr. [name]."* A concrete next step reduces the free-fall feeling.

Reflection: If you followed your patient home after discharge, would they know what to do? Would they feel ready? Or would they feel like they were just released?

"The appointment ended, but my worry didn't. I needed someone to check on me. Nobody did."
— Patient, 55

#25 DON'T FORGET ME AFTER I LEAVE — "THE VISIT ENDED. THE WORRY DIDN'T."

"After my appointment, I was told I'd get a call with my lab results. A week went by. Then two. I checked the portal every day — nothing. I finally called and sat on hold for twenty minutes. When someone answered, they said, 'Oh, those came back normal.' Just like that. Like it was nothing.

But it wasn't nothing to me. I'd spent two weeks convinced something was wrong. I'd barely slept. I almost called my sister to tell her I thought I was sick. And the whole time, my results were sitting somewhere and nobody thought to tell me.

It's not the waiting that hurt. It's that nobody seemed to realize I was waiting."

— Patient, 46

He told me that experience changed how he thinks about his care team.

"I trust my doctor in the room. But I don't trust the system once I leave the room. And that's a terrible feeling."

For patients, the visit doesn't end when they walk out the door. It ends when the uncertainty does.

There's a gap in healthcare that almost every patient has felt but few organizations have addressed: what happens after the visit. The exam room experience might be excellent — warm, thorough, personal. But the moment the patient walks out, they often enter a void. Test results that take days with no communication. Referrals that require the patient to chase down their appointment details. Follow-up calls that never come. Portal messages that go unanswered.

For providers, the post-visit period is operational. For patients, it's emotional. They're sitting at home replaying what the doctor said, searching their symptoms online, checking the portal obsessively, and interpreting silence as bad news. Every day without communication is a day the patient writes their own story — and it's usually a darker one than reality.

The follow-up gap is also where care plans fall apart. A patient leaves with good intentions and a printed plan, but without a check-in, without a nudge, without someone closing the loop, life takes over. The prescription doesn't get filled. The specialist doesn't get called. The lifestyle change doesn't stick. And three months later, the patient is back at square one, feeling like they failed — when really, the system just let go too soon.

This is where care coordinators, nurses, medical assistants, and even automated systems can make an enormous difference. A simple follow-up call —

"Just checking in. How are you doing since your visit?" —

communicates something no portal message can: You're still on our mind.

I watched one practice implement a 48-hour follow-up call for every patient who received difficult news. Just a two-minute phone call from a nurse. The impact was remarkable — patients described it as one of the most meaningful parts of their care.

"Nobody has ever called to check on me before," one woman said. *"It made me feel like I wasn't doing this alone."*

In practice:

- Set clear expectations before the patient leaves. *"Your results should be back by Thursday. If you don't hear from us by Friday, call this number."*
- Build a follow-up rhythm. A 48-hour check-in call after significant visits, procedures, or hard conversations.
- Don't let test results arrive without context. A result in a portal with no explanation creates anxiety. A sentence from a nurse — *"Your results look good, here's what they mean"* — creates relief.
- Close the referral loop. If you send a patient to a specialist, check that they got there. Patients fall through the cracks between organizations more than we realize.
- Designate a point of contact. Patients need to know who to call when they're confused after a visit — and it can't be a phone tree.

Reflection: After a patient leaves your care, does your system follow them — or forget them?

"I avoid the doctor now. Not because of the care. Because of the surprise. I can't afford to not know what something costs."
— Patient, 45

#26 DON'T LET THE BILL UNDO THE CARE — "THE SURPRISE UNDID EVERYTHING."

"Nobody told me what it was going to cost. Not even a ballpark. I asked at the front desk and they said, 'It depends on your insurance.' I asked the nurse and she said, 'You'd have to talk to billing.' I asked the doctor and he said, 'I don't really handle that side.' So I just went through with it and hoped for the best.

Three weeks later I got a bill for $2,400. I sat at my kitchen table and cried. Not because I couldn't afford it — though I couldn't — but because nobody had warned me. Nobody had given me the chance to ask questions or make a different choice. The visit itself was fine. But the bill erased all of it. That's all I remember now."

— Patient, 38

She told me she avoided going back for eight months. Not because of the care — because of the fear of another surprise.

"I needed follow-up. I knew I did. But every time I thought about calling, I felt that panic in my chest again."

Patients don't separate the clinical experience from the financial experience. To them, it's all one story — and the bill is often the final chapter.

This is one of the most overlooked parts of patient experience, and it's one of the most damaging. You can deliver flawless clinical care, build deep trust in the exam room, and send a patient home feeling seen and supported — and then a confusing, unexplained, or surprisingly large bill can undo all of it. In the patient's mind, the bill is part of the care. And when it feels predatory, careless, or opaque, it doesn't just cause financial stress. It causes a trust issue.

Patients talk about billing with the same language they use to describe clinical failures:

"I felt blindsided." "Nobody warned me." "I felt taken advantage of." "I'll never go back there."

The financial experience has become a clinical experience — because the anxiety, confusion, and anger it creates directly affects whether patients return, comply with treatment, or recommend your organization to others.

And here's what makes it worse: the people who handle billing are almost never included in patient experience training. They're seen as back-office, administrative, separate from *"care."* But to the patient calling with a confusing statement, overwhelmed and scared, the billing specialist is part of the care team. That voice on the phone is the organization. And the tone of that conversation — empathetic or dismissive, patient or rushed — will determine whether the patient's overall experience is remembered as caring or cold.

The providers reading this may feel like billing isn't their department. But patients don't think in departments.

And a two-sentence heads-up from a provider

— *"This might involve some out-of-pocket costs. Talk to our billing team before you leave so there are no surprises"* —

can prevent the kind of financial shock that drives patients away.

In practice:

- Normalize the cost conversation. Train clinical and front desk staff to proactively say, *"Let's make sure you understand the financial side before we move forward."*
- Create a financial navigator role or designate someone patients can talk to before procedures, not just after bills arrive.
- Train billing staff in empathetic communication. They're often talking to people who are scared, confused, and still recovering. Tone matters as much here as it does in the exam room.
- Simplify the bill. Use plain language. Show what was done, what it cost, what insurance covered, and what the patient owes — in a format a normal person can understand.
- Offer payment options proactively, not as a last resort after collections.

Reflection: If a patient described their entire experience with your organization — from the first phone call to the final bill — would the financial part make you proud or make you wince?

"She asked how my granddaughter was doing. The medicine mattered. But that moment mattered more."
— Patient, 66

#27 REMEMBER ME — "DON'T MAKE ME START FROM SCRATCH EVERY TIME."

"I came in expecting to pick up where we left off. Instead, I had to explain everything again — like the last visit never happened. It was frustrating, but also kind of discouraging."
— Patient, 29

To be remembered is to feel like you matter — even after you leave the room.

Being remembered is one of the quickest ways to make a patient feel valued. And the opposite is just as true. Patients get worn down by having to retell the same story, correct the same details, or reintroduce themselves like none of it stuck. Over time, that repetition doesn't just feel inefficient — it feels impersonal.

Patients aren't expecting perfect recall. They're expecting continuity. They want to feel like their history lives in the room, not just in the chart. When a provider remembers a detail — how work has been going, a child's name, the thing they were nervous about last time — it signals something deeper: you were paying attention, and you still are.

One patient put it bluntly: *"Every time I came in, it felt like I had to start over."*

Another described the difference when a provider said, *"How's your granddaughter doing?"* The medicine mattered, but the moment mattered too. It told them this relationship has memory.

Remembering doesn't require a photographic memory. It requires intention — reviewing the chart before you walk in, carrying forward a key detail, and using it to reduce friction and build trust. Small signals add up. They turn a system into a relationship.

In practice: Scan the chart before entering. Keep one or two *"continuity notes"* (what matters to them, what they're worried about, what's happening in their life). Start with a simple bridge: *"Last time you mentioned..."*

Reflection: Are patients repeating themselves - or is your process making them start over?

"They didn't lecture me for missing appointments. They just said, 'We're glad you're back."

— Patient, 30

#28 PERSISTENCE — "DON'T GIVE UP ON ME."

"I missed a few appointments and I started telling myself, 'They probably think I'm a problem patient.' I was already beating myself up, so the last thing I wanted was a lecture.

But when they called, it wasn't that. It was kind. It was simple. It was, 'Hey, we haven't seen you in a bit. How are you doing?' That call didn't fix everything, but it got me moving again."

— Patient, 41

He came back. He's been consistent for over a year now. He told me,

"That phone call was the difference. If they hadn't reached out, I would have just disappeared."

Patients fall off for a lot of reasons. Fear. Exhaustion. Money. Transportation. Depression. The feeling of *"I'm failing at this,"* especially when progress stalls. From the outside it can look like apathy. From the inside it's often overwhelming.

That's why persistence matters. A follow-up call after a missed appointment isn't just logistics. It's a signal. It tells the patient, *"You're not invisible. We're still here."*

And for someone who already feels behind, that can be the difference between disappearing and returning. The key is tone. Persistence isn't pressure. It's an open door. It's reaching out without judgment and making the next step easy.

In practice: Build a compassionate follow-up rhythm. Use language that assumes positive intent ("We missed you — want to get back on the schedule?"). Offer options. Remove friction. Keep the door open.

Reflection: Who has drifted away in your care — and what would it look like to reach out in a way that feels supportive, not shaming?

"Her excitement made me proud of myself. I didn't know I needed that until it happened."
— Patient, 52

#29 **CELEBRATE WITH ME —** "BE THERE WHEN I GET BETTER."

"I love and respect my doctor because he pays attention to the person, not just the numbers. I've been so stressed through this whole process, and most appointments feel pretty clinical.

But when the treatment started working, he was genuinely happy for me. He celebrated it with me like it mattered. And it did. I left feeling hopeful instead of just relieved."

— Patient, 36

That patient finished her treatment eight months later. She told me her doctor high-fived her at the final appointment.

"I took a picture of us," she said. "It's on my fridge."

Sometimes the most powerful thing a provider can do is say, 'Look how far you've come.

Healthcare is often associated with problems — what's wrong, what needs fixing, what hasn't improved yet. But patients also crave acknowledgment of progress. They want someone to celebrate with them when things get better, even in small ways.

Celebration doesn't need to be dramatic. It might be a high-five when a patient meets a goal, a handwritten note after surgery recovery, or a provider simply saying, "Look how far you've come." These moments remind patients that healing is a journey worth noticing, not just enduring.

One patient shared how their physical therapist clapped for them after they walked a few steps without pain.

"It sounds silly, but I felt like I had run a marathon. Her excitement made me proud of myself."

That pride became fuel for the next stage of healing.

In practice: Recognize progress out loud. Mark milestones. Celebrate not only outcomes but also effort.

Reflection: How often do you stop to acknowledge your patients' victories, large or small?

"One great appointment doesn't mean much if the next one feels like starting over."

— Patient, 61

#30 PERFORM — "BE CONSISTENT. BE EXCELLENT."

"I've had visits where the first appointment felt great, and then the next one felt totally different — rushed, distracted, like I had to start over. That messes with your confidence. It makes you wonder if you're actually being cared for, or if you just caught them on a 'good day.'

What stood out about this provider was how steady she was. First visit, tenth visit — it didn't matter. She came in prepared. She remembered the basics without me having to re-explain everything. She didn't make me feel like an interruption. And that consistency made me relax, because I felt like I was in good hands every single time."

— Patient, 37

Showing your humanity doesn't weaken your credibility. It's what earns it.

Patients are always scanning for signals that they're safe. Not in a dramatic way — more like a quiet running question in the background: Can I trust this? Can I trust you? A single "off" visit can shake that trust. Not because patients expect perfection, but because inconsistency makes the whole experience feel unpredictable.

Consistency is what turns care into confidence. When the tone, attention, and follow-through feel steady visit after visit, patients stop bracing. They stop re-litigating the basics. They're more likely to share what they've been holding back, and more likely to follow the plan because it feels dependable — not random.

Excellence isn't a single great day. It's the standard you hold when the day is heavy. Over time, that reliability becomes the foundation of loyalty. Patients come back because they know what they're walking into: the same level of preparedness, the same respect, the same intention.

In practice: Create simple repeatable habits that protect consistency — review the chart before you walk in, open with one grounding question, close with a clear next-step summary. Build team routines that reduce variability so your baseline stays high, even on hard days.

Reflection: If a patient only remembered the last time they saw you, would they describe you as steady — or hit-or-miss?

"He pushed the keyboard aside and said, 'Tell me what's going on.' I knew right then I was in the right place."
— Patient, 32

#31 PRIORITIZE — "DON'T LET THE SYSTEM GET IN THE WAY OF US."

"I started explaining what was wrong and they cut me off to finish paperwork. I get it — they have to document. But at that moment I felt like my story was an interruption."

— Patient, 48

A patient can handle a wait if they feel respected. What they can't handle is feeling invisible while the system hums along without them.

Patients can sense when the system comes first and they come second. Not because they don't understand workflow, but because they feel it in the tone. The rushed greeting. The clipped questions. The eyes locked on a screen while they're trying to explain something that scares them. When the process leads the visit, patients often pull back. They talk less. They trust less. They start to feel like they're being processed, not cared for.

The fix isn't pretending documentation doesn't exist. It's prioritizing the human moment inside the system. A patient can handle forms and delays if they feel oriented and respected. What they can't handle is feeling invisible while the system hums along without them.

Sometimes it's as small as a reset at the beginning.

"Hi. I'm glad you're here. Tell me what's going on." Or a quick acknowledgment: *"I'm going to ask a few computer questions first because I have to, but then I want to hear your story."*

That kind of transparency prevents patients from assuming they're not the priority.

This chapter isn't anti-system. It's pro-relationship. Patients remember when someone pushed the keyboard aside, even briefly, and treated them like the most important thing in the room.

In practice: Lead with the person, not the portal. Start with one human question before turning to documentation. If tasks must come first, name it and come back to the patient quickly. When you return, show it: eye contact, a pause, and a summary of what you heard.

Reflection: Where does the system routinely hijack your visit — and what could you do, even for 30 seconds, to put the patient back at the center?

"I didn't know what to watch for. But I could feel that she was watching for me."
— Patient, 62

#32 **KEEP ME SAFE** — "LET ME KNOW YOU'VE GOT ME."

"They noticed something I didn't, and it protected me."
— Patient, 49

Patients can't always tell you what's wrong. But they always know when someone is paying attention.

Safety isn't just a protocol. It's a feeling patients carry — or don't — through every step of care. Most patients can't evaluate your technical skill, and they don't know which details matter medically. But they know when someone is paying attention. They know when they're being handled versus cared for. They know when the room feels steady.

A lot of safety comes down to diagnosing the person, not just the problem. Patients show up with a chief complaint, but they also show up with context — stress, sleep loss, fear, confusion, medication side effects, family pressure, work demands, past experiences. They often don't know what's relevant, so they share what feels obvious and leave out what feels *"small."* That's where attentive care becomes protective. The clinician who notices they're short of breath while talking. The nurse who catches hesitation and asks the second question.

The provider who sees the guarded posture and asks,

"What are you trying not to do because it hurts?"

Those moments aren't just good bedside manner. They prevent missed information and missed diagnoses.

And safety lives in the quiet details patients can't always name. The moment you notice they're nodding but not tracking. The moment you realize they're minimizing symptoms because they don't want to be *"dramatic."* The moment you catch that the story doesn't quite match the timeline. When you slow down and connect the dots, patients feel protected — not because you said *"you're safe,"* but because your attention proves it.

This kind of safety is visible. It sounds like,

"Let me make sure I understand."

It looks like a pause before moving on. It feels like someone taking the time to double-check without acting annoyed. It turns the experience from

"I hope nothing gets missed" into *"They've got me."*

Yes, checklists matter. But what patients remember most is the vigilance they could feel: the sense that someone was watching out for them when they didn't even know what to watch for.

In practice:

- Start by seeing the whole person. Ask one context question: *"What has this been like for you day to day?"*
- Ask the second question. When you hear *"I'm fine,"* try *"Help me understand that."*
- Watch for confusion. Use teach-back: *"What are you going to do when you get home?"*
- Make your carefulness visible. Say what you're checking and why.
- Invite interruption. *"If anything feels off, tell me right away."*

Reflection: When patients leave your care, do they feel like you treated a symptom — or like you truly saw them and protected what might have been missed?

"The ER team knew my story. They'd been kind. Then I got wheeled upstairs and suddenly nobody knew anything."
— Patient, 59

#33 **THE HANDOFF** — "DON'T DROP ME BETWEEN DEPARTMENTS."

"I went from the ER to a hospital room, and it felt like I went from one world to another. The ER team knew my story. They knew what I was afraid of. They'd been kind. Then I got wheeled upstairs and suddenly nobody knew anything. The nurse asked me the same questions the ER had already asked. The doctor came in and introduced himself like we were starting from zero. I thought, didn't anyone tell them?

I felt like a package that got delivered to the wrong address. The people were nice enough. But the thread was gone. Whatever trust I'd built downstairs didn't come upstairs with me."

— Patient, 59

He told me later that the disconnect made him doubt whether the teams were even coordinating his treatment.

If they can't pass along my story, how do I know they're passing along my medications?

"When patients move between teams, they shouldn't feel like they're starting over. The relationship should travel with them."

In healthcare, transitions happen constantly — from the ER to the floor, from one shift to the next, from the hospital to a rehab facility, from a primary care doctor to a specialist. Inside the system, these are operational handoffs. For patients, they're emotional cliffs.

Every transition is a moment where trust is either carried forward or dropped. When a patient has spent an hour building rapport with one team, opening up about their fears, explaining their story — and then gets moved to a new team that knows none of it — the message is clear: what just happened didn't matter enough to follow you here.

I've watched this play out dozens of times. A patient builds trust with an ER nurse, finally relaxes, finally feels safe — and then gets transferred to a floor where nobody acknowledges what came before. The patient doesn't just feel inconvenienced. They feel erased. And they start over guarded, sharing less, trusting less.

The best handoffs I've witnessed aren't just clinical — they're relational. I once watched a nurse walk a patient to the next unit herself, introduce her to the receiving nurse by name, and say in front of the patient,

"This is Mrs. Rodriguez. She's been really worried about the biopsy results, and she has a daughter in college who's been calling every hour. She likes to know what's happening before it happens."

That took about forty-five seconds. And it told the patient: you're not starting over. Your story came with you.

Patients don't experience departments. They experience one continuous relationship with your organization. When the handoff breaks that continuity, patients feel dropped — even if the clinical care is seamless.

In practice:

- Brief the receiving team on the person, not just the case. One human detail carried forward — what they're worried about, who's in the waiting room, what calms them down — changes everything.
- Introduce the next team before you leave. When possible, walk the patient to the next point of care and make a warm introduction.
- Tell the patient what's going to happen in the transition. *"The night team is coming on at seven. I've told them about you and what we're working on."*
- Use bedside handoff when possible. Let the patient hear the transfer of information. It builds confidence that nothing is being lost.

Reflection: When your patients move to the next team, do they feel carried forward — or started over?

"We kept thinking, surely someone is coordinating this. But the reality felt like a baton drop."
— Family Member

#34 CLOSE THE LOOP — "SAY IT THE SAME WAY EVERY TIME."

"What made it worse wasn't even the medical situation. It was the feeling that nobody was talking to each other.

The ER handed us paperwork and made it sound final. The ICU felt like they were operating off a different story. We were trying to advocate, but we didn't know which version was 'real.' We were scared to ask too many questions because we didn't want to be labeled difficult — yet we could feel that the plan was drifting.

We kept thinking, surely someone is coordinating this. But the reality felt like a baton drop. Information wasn't moving cleanly. Expectations weren't aligned. And in the middle of all of it was a human being who couldn't breathe well and a family trying to make the right call.

When the consult finally happened, things got clear. But the clarity came late. It should not take a next-day consult for everyone to understand the decision the same way."

— Family Member

Patients don't experience *"departments."* They experience one continuous story. When the story breaks — when the message changes by hallway, shift, or unit — trust collapses fast.

Inside healthcare operations, we call this handoffs, transitions, throughput, interdisciplinary alignment. Patients call it something simpler: "I don't feel safe."

When the ER, ICU, inpatient team, consult services, and nursing are not operating from the same shared mental model, families feel like they're doing project management in a crisis. And the cost is real: confusion, duplicated conversations, delayed decisions, moral distress, and sometimes preventable harm.

Closing the loop isn't a *"soft skill."* It's an execution discipline. It's one of the cleanest ways to convert compassion into reliability.

In practice (closed-loop communication that patients can feel):

- Name the owner of the plan. Families need to know who is accountable for aligning the team.
- Standardize the handoff, especially for code status / goals-of-care. If you use SBAR or a similar framework internally, translate the bottom line for families: *"Here's what we agreed on. Here's what happens next."*
- Do a same-day touchpoint when decisions are made late. If a consult can't happen until tomorrow, don't leave families in overnight ambiguity. A five-minute alignment check can change everything.
- Make documentation actionable. *"Documented"* is not the same as *"communicated."* Ensure the plan is visible in the chart where downstream teams actually look.
- Invite correction. *"If you hear something different from anyone on our team, please tell us immediately — because we want one clear message."*

Reflection: If a patient's life depends on the plan being executed consistently across teams, are you building a system where alignment is assumed — or engineered?

"People were acting like they knew, without verifying. We were the ones fact-checking while terrified."
— Family Member

#35 VERIFY BEFORE YOU TREAT — "VERIFY ALWAYS. ASSUME NEVER."

"I watched them give breathing treatments like the problem was asthma. But it wasn't asthma. It was a narrowing airway.

The family was asking questions because what they were seeing didn't match what they were being told. One nurse told us a certain procedure had been done overnight while we were gone. Then the doctor came in and it became clear that wasn't accurate. Later, a nurse who was also a family member stepped in and advocated for a different treatment — the one that actually fit what was happening.

That moment broke something in me. Not because mistakes never happen. But because the confidence in the room didn't match the reality. People were acting like they knew, without verifying. And the chart — the actual source of truth — didn't seem to be driving the decisions or the communication.

It felt like the care plan was being built on assumptions, and we were the ones trying to fact-check it while terrified."
— Family Member

There's a specific kind of fear that shows up when families sense the team is *"moving"* but not necessarily *"seeing."* When care becomes activity instead of accuracy, patients don't feel cared for — they feel handled.

This is where communication and clinical excellence intersect. Because verifying isn't only clinical. It's relational. When you say something happened and it didn't, the patient doesn't just question that detail. They start questioning everything: Did anyone review the chart? Are we treating the real problem? Is the team aligned? If we weren't here, would anyone catch this?

The best teams don't just *"do things."* They operate with discipline: verify before you speak, verify before you treat, verify before you reassure.

And when something is unclear, they narrate their thinking out loud. That transparency lowers panic, increases trust, and often surfaces the missing detail faster than silence ever will.

In practice:

- Default to the chart plus the bedside, not hearsay. If you're not sure, say so — then verify.
- Use a *"pause point"* when the story doesn't fit. *"Something here isn't matching — let's stop and reconcile the facts."*
- Document and communicate in the same breath. If you tell the family, make sure the record matches and the next team will see it.
- Repair fast when misinformation happens. *"I need to correct something I said earlier. Here's what is true, and here's what we're doing now."* That kind of honesty is stabilizing.
- Invite family observations as data, not disruption. *"What are you noticing that concerns you?"* Families often see pattern changes first.

Reflection: When a family is scared and watching closely, does your communication create confidence because you're certain — or because you're transparent and verifying?

"They called me 'the hip in room four.' After that, I second-guessed every interaction."
— Patient, 71

#36 THE HIP IN ROOM FOUR — "WHAT I OVERHEARD CHANGED EVERYTHING."

"I overheard two nurses talking about me in the hallway. They didn't say anything cruel. But the way they referred to me — 'the hip in room four' — made my stomach drop. I wasn't a person to them. I was a body part and a room number.

After that, I second-guessed every interaction. When someone smiled at me, I wondered if they were being genuine or just professional. It changed how I felt about the whole stay. Not because of what they said to my face — because of what they said when they thought I couldn't hear."

— Patient, 71

He told me he never complained.

"What would I even say? 'I heard you calling me a hip'? They'd think I was being ridiculous. But it stuck with me. It's been two years and I still think about it."

The way your team talks about patients when patients aren't around is the truest measure of your culture.

This is the chapter that might make some people uncomfortable. But it's one of the most important things I've observed in over a decade of spending time inside healthcare facilities:

the way staff talk about patients when they think no one is listening tells you everything about the culture of that organization.

Most of the time, it's not malicious. It's shorthand.

"The hip in room four." "The frequent flier in the ER." "The difficult family in bed seven."

These labels develop naturally in high-pressure environments where efficiency matters and emotional distance can feel protective. But patients hear them. Families hear them. And when they do, it fundamentally changes how they experience their care.

I've stood in hallways and heard staff discuss patients with genuine compassion —

"I'm really worried about her, she seems scared, let's make sure we check on her tonight."

And I've stood in the same hallways and heard language that would devastate the patient if they overheard it. The difference isn't about individual character. It's about culture. It's about what's normalized, what's tolerated, and what leadership models.

Here's why this matters operationally, not just morally: how you talk about patients when they're not around shapes how you treat them when they are. Language creates lens. If someone is *"the hip in room four,"* the team approaches them as a task. If they're *"Mrs. Chen, the retired teacher who's nervous about anesthesia,"* the team approaches them as a person.

Clinical care may be identical, but the patient experience is what truly lasts. For families, trust is fragile: casual language can instantly turn confidence into lasting suspicion.

In practice:

- Use names, not room numbers or diagnoses, when speaking directly with patients and in private clinical settings. *"Mrs. Chen in room four"* instead of *"the hip in four."* It takes one second longer and changes the entire framework.
- Leaders: model the language you want to hear. If the charge nurse refers to patients by name, the team will follow.
- Create a culture where someone can gently correct without backlash. *"Hey — that's Mr. Torres"* should feel normal, not confrontational.
- Assume every conversation can be overheard. Hallways, nursing stations, break rooms near patient areas — sound travels. Speak accordingly.
- Remember that families are always listening. Even when they look asleep in the corner chair, they're absorbing the tone and language of every person who walks in.

Reflection: If your patients could hear every conversation your team has about them — in the hallway, at the nursing station, during handoff — would they feel respected? Would they still trust you?

"The convenience was great. The connection wasn't. I could tell she was multitasking."
— Patient, 30

#37 THE SCREEN BETWEEN US — "SOMETHING WAS MISSING."

"I appreciate that I can do virtual visits now. I really do. But there's something about it that feels... thinner. Like the connection has to work harder to get through the screen.

My doctor is great in person. She's warm, she listens, she makes me feel seen. But on video, I felt like I was talking to someone at a call center. She was looking at me, but it didn't feel like eye contact. There were pauses that felt awkward instead of comfortable. And when the visit was over, she clicked a button and I was staring at my own reflection. No walk to the checkout desk. No smile from the receptionist on the way out. Just me, alone, in my kitchen, trying to process what she said.

I'm not saying telehealth is bad. I'm saying it needs its own version of warmth. Because the convenience is great — but the connection can't just disappear because there's a screen involved."

— Patient, 34

She told me she now does a mix of virtual and in-person visits.

"I save the hard conversations for in-person. For the check-ins, video is fine — as long as they still show up like they mean it."

The screen can connect you or separate you. Which one it does depends on how you show up.

Telehealth is here to stay. And for many patients, it's been a genuine improvement — less travel, less time off work, less sitting in waiting rooms. For patients in rural areas, for those with mobility challenges, for parents juggling childcare, virtual visits can be a lifeline.

But telehealth also introduces a new set of connection challenges that most providers have never been trained for. The body language that builds trust in person — leaning in, turning toward the patient, the subtle nod — is largely invisible on a screen. Eye contact is nearly impossible because looking at the patient's face means looking away from the camera. The natural rhythm of conversation gets disrupted by audio delays. And the visit ends with a click instead of a handshake.

Patients notice all of this. They describe virtual visits as *"efficient but cold," "fine but forgettable," or "like talking to someone who's sort of there."* The warmth that comes naturally in person has to be intentionally engineered on screen. That's not a criticism of telehealth — it's a design challenge. And it's solvable.

The providers who do telehealth well do a few things differently. They open with warmth, just like they would in person:

"I'm glad we could connect today. How have you been?" They narrate what they're doing: "I'm looking at your chart right now — give me just a second."

They look at the camera when they're listening, not at the screen. And they close with something human: *"I'm here if you need anything before our next visit. Don't hesitate to reach out."*

The post-visit experience matters even more in telehealth because there's no physical transition — no checkout, no scheduling at the front desk, no human goodbye. A follow-up message, a summary of the plan, or even a simple *"Thank you for meeting with me today"* can replace the warmth that the hallway used to provide.

In practice:

- Open with connection, not clinical business. *"How are you doing?" before "What brings you in?"* matters even more on screen.
- Look at the camera when listening. It's unnatural, but it's the closest thing to eye contact on video.
- Narrate your actions. *"I'm reviewing your labs now"* prevents the awkward silence that patients interpret as disengagement.
- Minimize distractions. Close other tabs. Mute notifications. Patients can tell when you're multitasking — and on screen, it's even more obvious.
- Close the visit warmly and follow up in writing. A portal message summarizing the plan replaces the checkout interaction patients are used to.
- Ask patients how the virtual format is working for them. Some conversations need to be in person. Give patients permission to say so.

Reflection: On your last virtual visit, did the patient feel connected to you — or just connected to the internet?

PART III — THE IMPACT OF LISTENING & LEADING

MORE THAN MEDICINE

The moments that change everything don't cost more money. They cost more attention.

When patients shared their stories, they weren't asking for perfection. They weren't asking for the newest technology, a longer appointment, or a miracle cure. Over and over, they asked for something simpler — and harder to sustain in a busy system.

They wanted to feel seen. They wanted to feel safe. They wanted to feel like they mattered.

They talked about presence. About dignity. About honesty. About hope. Not as *"nice extras,"* but as the difference between opening up and shutting down. Between following a plan and quietly giving up on it. Between returning and never coming back.

And trust — real trust — has a target. Patients are deciding whether they can trust the person in front of them with their fear, their body, their story, their future. They're also deciding whether they can trust the team and the system behind that person to carry them forward without dropping them. Do you remember them? Will you follow through? Will anyone notice when they're confused, overwhelmed, or minimizing what's really going on?

This is what makes these requests feel small on paper and enormous in real life. A glance at a watch. A rushed tone. A provider who doesn't read the chart. A plan that ignores real life. These aren't minor to a patient. They are signals. And patients build their behavior around the signals they receive.

Here's the paradox. The moments that change the experience don't cost more money. They cost more attention. They require a willingness to slow down for ten seconds, ask one more question, and treat the person — not the problem.

That's what patients were asking for. Not more medicine. More humanity.

A moment of real connection in an exam room almost never stays contained. It travels.

For the patient, it lowers the guard. Trust rises. Anxiety eases. They share more. They ask the question they almost didn't ask. And when people feel heard, they're more likely to follow the plan and stay engaged long enough for healing to take hold.

For the family, it becomes a sentence they repeat for years: *"They treated us like we mattered."* Those stories move faster than marketing ever will. They show up at dinner tables, in group texts, in waiting rooms, and in the choices people make when they decide where to go next.

For the provider, it brings meaning back. Burnout often grows where care becomes transactional — when the work is all volume and no relationship. Connection restores the *"why."* It's often the part of the day that reminds clinicians they're not just managing problems — they're helping people.

For the team, it sets the tone. A workplace that protects dignity and models respect doesn't just create better patient experiences — it creates better team experiences. The way staff speak to each other behind the scenes becomes the way patients feel treated on the front lines. Culture is never neutral. It leaks.

And the ripple keeps going — into the organization, into the community, into the experiences patients share with family, friends and online. Connection is contagious.

LISTENING AS LEADERSHIP

In healthcare, leadership isn't proven by how many decisions you make. It's proven by whether people feel heard when they're speaking to you. Titles can create authority, but listening creates alignment — and alignment is what turns a busy organization into a trusted one.

When leaders listen to their teams, staff stop feeling like replaceable labor and start feeling like owners of the mission. They speak up earlier. They flag risks sooner. They share what's breaking in workflows, what's confusing patients, what's draining morale, and what's quietly eroding quality. Listening doesn't just boost culture — it improves safety. It catches problems before they become patterns.

And teams take their cues from what leadership rewards. If the culture says, Keep your head down and hit the numbers, staff learn to survive the day. If the culture says, Your voice matters, staff learn to invest in the work. People who feel respected tend to extend respect. They slow down for the patient who's overwhelmed. They explain instead of dismiss. They follow up instead of letting someone drift away. That's not soft. That's operational.

Patients feel the difference immediately. Not in mission statements — in moments. In whether they're interrupted. In whether someone notices confusion. In whether the plan fits real life. When patients feel listened to, they trust the care more, share more truth, and follow through more consistently. They return, not just because the care was competent, but because the relationship felt safe. And they tell other people. Trust multiplies.

Healthcare has long been measured in numbers: infection rates, length of stay, readmissions, throughput, productivity. Those metrics matter. They protect patients. They guide improvement. They keep systems accountable. But they don't tell the whole story — because patients don't experience care as a spreadsheet. They experience it as a moment in their life when they're vulnerable and trying to trust the people in front of them.

When we align clinical outcomes with human outcomes, performance gets stronger. Not just because workflows are optimized, but because trust changes behavior. Trust increases disclosure. It increases follow-through. It reduces no-shows. It improves adherence. Hope keeps patients engaged long enough for treatment to work. And relationships create the conditions where healing is more likely — not only physically, but emotionally and socially, where recovery actually lives.

This is the business case and the moral case meeting in the same place. The best marketing strategy isn't a campaign. It's consistency in the exam room. The strongest reputation isn't bought. It's earned in thousands of small moments patients repeat to other people. Sustainable growth doesn't start with visibility. It starts with experience.

THE COURAGE TO CARE

The question isn't whether we have time to connect. The question is whether we have the courage. Because connection in healthcare isn't hard because it's complicated. It's hard because it costs something in the moment — attention, humility, emotional presence — especially when the schedule is tight and the system is loud.

It takes courage to pause at the doorway and enter the room like the person matters more than the pace. Courage to notice what's underneath the symptoms. Courage to ask the second question when *"I'm fine"* sounds practiced. Courage to sit in the silence without rescuing it. Courage to say, *"I don't know yet, but I will stay with you until we do."* Courage to admit, *"That would be hard for me too,"* without making the moment about you. Courage to prioritize the human being over the process — without pretending the process doesn't exist. And it takes courage to listen.

Because listening isn't passive. It's an intervention. It changes what gets revealed. It changes what gets diagnosed. It changes what patients are willing to admit, what families are willing to share, and what teams are willing to surface before problems become harmful.

Listening disrupts autopilot. It interrupts assumptions. It slows the room down just enough to make care safer, kinder, and more accurate.

Over time, that kind of listening changes more than a single encounter. It shapes culture. It sets expectations. It teaches teams what matters here. It pulls people back from burnout by restoring meaning. It builds reputations the right way — through lived experience, not branding.

Imagine what would happen if every provider, every team, every leader embraced this call: to listen more deeply, to connect more intentionally, to treat every patient as if they were the only one in the room.

Patients would feel safe, valued, and hopeful. Families would carry stories of respect and care into their communities. Teams would rediscover joy in their work. Organizations would grow — not just in numbers, but in trust.

This isn't a dream. It's possible. Patients have told us exactly what they need. The blueprint is in their words. The responsibility to act is ours.

Let us be the generation that makes healthcare human again. Let us listen — not just with our ears, but with our presence, our courage, and our hearts.

Because in the end, patients don't remember every chart, every scan, every statistic. They remember how we made them feel. And that feeling — that connection — can change everything.

Listening is the intervention. It always has been.

THE CHALLENGE

You have heard the voices of patients. You have seen what they long for: presence, honesty, dignity, respect, partnership, and hope. None of these require new technology, extra funding, or more degrees. They require choice. Daily choice.

So here is the challenge:

- **For the next 30 days, choose one act of intentional connection in every encounter.** It might be a pause at the doorway, eye contact before speaking, a patient's name spoken with warmth, or a question asked twice because the first answer didn't feel complete. It doesn't have to be big. It must be real.
- **Listen before you explain.** Patients have told us: they want to be heard. Give them space before you rush into the plan.
- **See the person, not the chart.** Remember one detail about who they are outside of the exam room. A hobby. A family member. A dream. Let them know you see their humanity.
- **Give encouragement freely.** A simple *"You're doing well"* or *"I'm proud of you"* can carry someone further than you imagine.

- **Reflect each day.** At the end of your shift, ask yourself: Who felt truly seen today because of me?

Thirty days. Thirty small choices. Thirty moments of connection that ripple outward.

If every provider, nurse, receptionist, and leader took this challenge, the culture of healthcare would shift. Patients would feel it. Families would talk about it. Teams would thrive in it. And reputations would grow because of it.

This isn't theory. It's practice. It begins now, with you. The challenge is simple. The impact is profound. The only question is: will you choose to connect?

Scan my QR Code for your 30-Day Connection Nudges — one small, specific action for each day. You can sign up for email or SMS text reminders.

REFLECTIONS

REFERENCES

- Agency for Healthcare Research and Quality. 2024. AHRQ Health Literacy Universal Precautions Toolkit. 3rd ed. Rockville, MD: Agency for Healthcare Research and Quality.
- Ambady, Nalini, and Robert Rosenthal. 1992. "Thin Slices of Expressive Behavior as Predictors of Interpersonal Consequences: A Meta-Analysis." Psychological Bulletin 111 (2): 256–274. doi:10.1037/0033-2909.111.2.256.
- Balik, Bridget, John Conway, Leah Zipperer, and Julie Watson. 2011. Achieving an Exceptional Patient and Family Experience of Inpatient Hospital Care. IHI Innovation Series White Paper. Cambridge, MA: Institute for Healthcare Improvement.
- Beckman, Howard B., and Richard M. Frankel. 1984. "The Effect of Physician Behavior on the Collection of Data." Annals of Internal Medicine 101 (5): 692–696. doi:10.7326/0003-4819-101-5-692.
- Centers for Medicare & Medicaid Services. n.d. HCAHPS: Patients' Perspectives of Care Survey. Accessed January 23, 2026.
- Centers for Medicare & Medicaid Services. 2025. Hospital CAHPS (HCAHPS). Accessed January 23, 2026.
- Committee on Quality of Health Care in America, Institute of Medicine. 2001. Crossing the Quality Chasm: A New Health System for the 21st Century. Washington, DC: National Academies Press.

- Elwyn, Glyn, Marie Anne Durand, Julia Song, Johanna Aarts, Paul J. Barr, Zackary Berger, et al. 2017. "A Three-Talk Model for Shared Decision Making: Multistage Consultation Process." BMJ 359: j4891. doi:10.1136/bmj.j4891.
- Greene-Moton, Ella, and Meredith Minkler. 2020. "Cultural Competence or Cultural Humility? Moving Beyond the Debate." Health Promotion Practice 21 (1): 142–145. doi:10.1177/1524839919884912.
- Institute for Healthcare Improvement. 2011. Achieving an Exceptional Patient and Family Experience of Inpatient Hospital Care. Cambridge, MA: Institute for Healthcare Improvement.
- Institute for Healthcare Improvement. n.d. Always Use Teach-Back! Accessed January 23, 2026.
- Institute for Healthcare Improvement. n.d. "To Prevent Patient Harm, Practice Respect and Deliver Dignity." Accessed January 23, 2026.
- Shanafelt, Tait D. 2009. "Enhancing Meaning in Work: A Prescription for Preventing Physician Burnout and Promoting Patient-Centered Care." JAMA 302 (12): 1338–1340.
- Snyder, C. R. 1994. The Psychology of Hope: You Can Get There from Here. New York: Free Press.
- Tabata-Kelly, Masami, et al. 2024. "The Paradox of Burnout From Physicians' Most Meaningful Roles." JAMA Network Open.
- Tervalon, Melanie, and Jann Murray-García. 1998. "Cultural Humility Versus Cultural Competence: A Critical Distinction in Defining Physician Training Outcomes in Multicultural Education." Journal of Health Care for the Poor and Underserved 9 (2): 117–125.
- Willis, Janine, and Alexander Todorov. 2006. "First Impressions: Making Up Your Mind After a 100-ms Exposure to a Face." Psychological Science 17 (7): 592–598.

The patient and family member quotes in this book are drawn from real interviews, reviews, and surveys conducted over more than a decade. Names and identifying details have been changed to protect privacy. Ages are approximate and are used for attribution purposes only.
This book is intended for educational and informational purposes and does not constitute medical advice.

CONNECT

THE PATIENT'S VOICE:

LISTENING, LEADING, AND TRANSFORMING CARE

www.ingramcontent.com/pod-product-compliance
Lightning Source LLC
LaVergne TN
LVHW022202200926
848481LV00006B/1818